Producer & International Distributor
eBookPro Publishing
www.ebook-pro.com

PASSOVER HAGGADAH – THE NO-NONSENSE HAGGADAH:
The Essential Family-Friendly Traditional Passover Haggadah for a Meaningful and Speedy Seder

MILAH TOVAH PRESS
Copyright © 2023 Made easy press

All rights reserved; No parts of this book may be reproduced or transmitted in any form or by any means, electronic or mechanical, including photocopying, recording, taping, or by any information retrieval system, without the permission, in writing, of the author.

Cover & Illustrations: Maria Sokhatski
Editor: Dani Silas

Contact: agency@ebook-pro.com

HOW TO USE THIS HAGGADAH

The No-Nonsense Haggadah was designed to give the modern Jewish family a solution to the long-winded and often confusing Haggadahs of tradition.

We've taken all the essentials of the Haggadah, presented them in a shortened and simplified way, and packed it all up into a clean, aesthetically pleasing package.

With Hebrew text followed by English transliterations and full translations, the festival of Passover has never been easier to enjoy. Perfect for families and participants of all ages, **The No-Nonsense Haggadah** makes Passover a true delight.

Icons alongside the text will help orient you and clarify what needs to be done next:

   Appears next to instructions

   Lets you know when a blessing should be recited

   Appears in relation to the four cups of wine

Also, you will find additional songs and texts in the appendix for the complete experience and for those of you who may wish to keep the evening more traditional.

If there will be children at your Passover Seder night, make sure to take a look at our children's version of the Haggadah – The Passover Haggadah for Kids. The text and layout are the same as in this book, so that kids can follow along easily, but this special Haggadah includes fun activities and work pages to keep children engaged and occupied throughout the night.

THE ORDER OF THE SEDER

7   **KADESH** — Blessing on the Wine
13 **URCHATZ** — Washing Hands
14 **KARPAS** — The Leafy Vegetable
17 **YACHATZ** — Breaking the Middle Matzah
19 **MAGID** — Telling the Story of Exodus
39 **RACHTZAH** — Washing Hands (this time, with a blessing)
41 **MOTZI-MATZAH** — Blessing on the Matzah
43 **MAROR** — Bitter Herb
45 **KORECH** — Maror Wrapped in Matzah
47 **SHULCHAN-ORECH** — The Festive Meal
49 **TZAFUN** — The Afikoman
51 **BARECH** — Blessing After the Meal
55 **HALLEL** — Praise to G-d
59 **NIRTZAH** — Conclusion of the Seder
61 **SONGS**
71 **APPENDIX** — Additions

THE SEDER PLATE

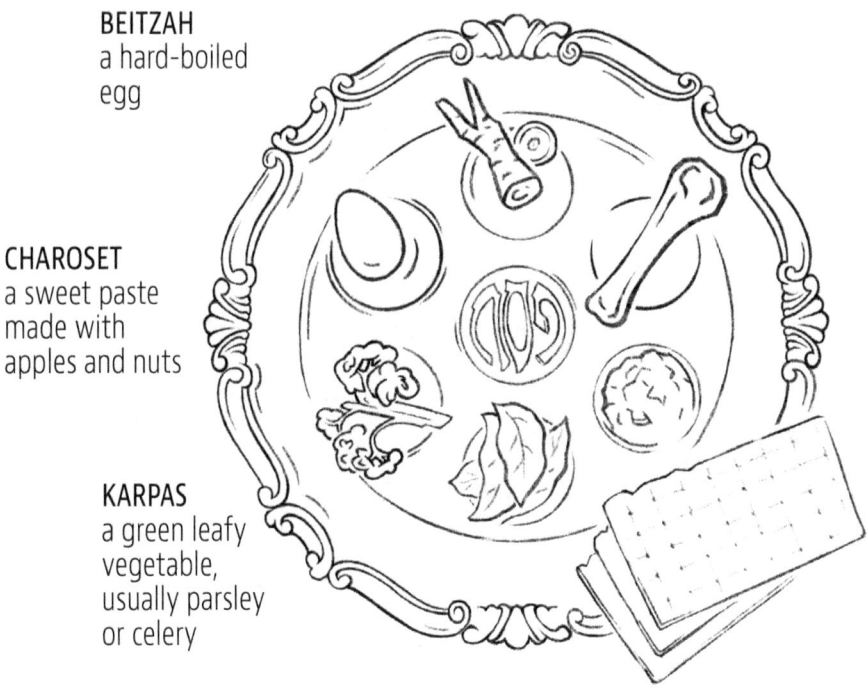

ZERO'A
typically a lamb shank bone, often substituted for cooked chicken

MAROR
a bitter vegetable, usually horseradish or lettuce

BEITZAH
a hard-boiled egg

CHAROSET
a sweet paste made with apples and nuts

KARPAS
a green leafy vegetable, usually parsley or celery

HAZERET
more of the same or a different bitter vegetable

MATZAH
beside the seder plate, we place three whole matzahs, which will play an important part in the seder

KADESH קַדֵּשׁ

Blessing on the Wine

KADESH קַדֵּשׁ

   Pour everyone a first full cup of wine.

   Recite the Kiddush blessing, adding the parentheses when the Seder falls on the Sabbath:

וַיְהִי עֶרֶב וַיְהִי בֹקֶר יוֹם הַשִּׁשִּׁי. וַיְכֻלּוּ הַשָּׁמַיִם וְהָאָרֶץ וְכָל צְבָאָם. וַיְכַל אֱלֹהִים בַּיּוֹם הַשְּׁבִיעִי מְלַאכְתּוֹ אֲשֶׁר עָשָׂה וַיִּשְׁבֹּת בַּיּוֹם הַשְּׁבִיעִי מִכָּל מְלַאכְתּוֹ אֲשֶׁר עָשָׂה. וַיְבָרֶךְ אֱלֹהִים אֶת יוֹם הַשְּׁבִיעִי וַיְקַדֵּשׁ אוֹתוֹ כִּי בוֹ שָׁבַת מִכָּל מְלַאכְתּוֹ אֲשֶׁר בָּרָא אֱלֹהִים לַעֲשׂוֹת.

Vayehi erev, vayehi voker, yom ha-shishi. V'yechulu ha-shamayim v'ha'aretz v'chol tzeva'am. V'yechal Elohim ba-yom ha-shevi'i mi-kol melachto asher asah, v'yishbot ba-yom ha-shvi'i mi-kol melachto asher asah. V'yevarech Elohim et yom ha-shvi'i v'yekadesh oto, ki vo shavat mi-kol melachto asher bara Elohim la'asot.

And so it was evening, and so it was morning, the sixth day. And G-d had completed the skies and the earth and all their host. And on the seventh day, G-d finished His work which He had done, and on the seventh day G-d rested from the work which He had done. And G-d blessed the seventh day and sanctified it, for on that day He rested from His work and all that He had done.

בָּרוּךְ אַתָּה יְיָ אֱלֹהֵינוּ מֶלֶךְ הָעוֹלָם בּוֹרֵא פְּרִי הַגָּפֶן.

Baruch atah Adonai, Eloheinu melech ha-olam, borei peri ha-gafen.

Blessed are You, Lord our G-d, King of the universe, creator of the fruit of the vine.

בָּרוּךְ אַתָּה יְיָ אֱלֹהֵינוּ מֶלֶךְ הָעוֹלָם, אֲשֶׁר בָּחַר בָּנוּ מִכָּל עָם וְרוֹמְמָנוּ מִכָּל לָשׁוֹן וְקִדְּשָׁנוּ בְּמִצְוֹתָיו. וַתִּתֶּן לָנוּ יְיָ אֱלֹהֵינוּ בְּאַהֲבָה (בְּשַׁבָּת: שַׁבָּתוֹת לִמְנוּחָה וּ) מוֹעֲדִים לְשִׂמְחָה, חַגִּים וּזְמַנִּים לְשָׂשׂוֹן, אֶת יוֹם (הַשַּׁבָּת הַזֶּה וְאֶת יוֹם) חַג הַמַּצּוֹת הַזֶּה, זְמַן חֵרוּתֵנוּ (בְּאַהֲבָה), מִקְרָא קֹדֶשׁ, זֵכֶר לִיצִיאַת מִצְרָיִם. כִּי בָנוּ בָחַרְתָּ וְאוֹתָנוּ קִדַּשְׁתָּ מִכָּל הָעַמִּים, (וְשַׁבָּת) וּמוֹעֲדֵי קָדְשֶׁךָ (בְּאַהֲבָה וּבְרָצוֹן,) בְּשִׂמְחָה וּבְשָׂשׂוֹן הִנְחַלְתָּנוּ. בָּרוּךְ אַתָּה יְיָ, מְקַדֵּשׁ (הַשַּׁבָּת וְ)יִשְׂרָאֵל וְהַזְּמַנִּים.

Baruch atah Adonai, Eloheinu melech ha-olam, asher bachar banu mi-kol 'am v'romemanu mi-kol lashon v'kideshanu b'mitzvotav. V'titen lanu Adonai Eloheinu b'ahava (shabbatot li-mnucha v') mo'adim l'-simcha, chagim uzmanim l'sason, et yom (ha-shabbat hazeh ve'et yom) chag ha-matzot hazeh, zman cheruteinu (b'ahava) mikra kodesh, Zecher l'yetziyat mitzrayim. Ki banu bacharta v'otanu kidashta mi-kol ha-amim, (v'shabbat) umo'adei kodshecha (b'ahava uvratzon,) b'simcha uvsason hinchaltanu. Baruch atah Adonai, mekadesh (ha-shabbat v') Yisrael v'ha-zmanim.

Blessed are you, Lord our G-d, King of the universe, who has chosen us among all people and raised us above all languages, and sanctified us through His commandments. The Lord our G-d has lovingly given us (the Shabbat to rest, and) festivals to be joyful, holidays and special times for gladness, this (Shabbat day and this) Passover, our time of (loving) freedom, in holiness and in memory of the Exodus from Egypt. For us You have chosen and us You have sanctified from all the people, and You have (lovingly and willingly) given us (Shabbat and) the holy times for happiness and joy. Blessed are You, G-d, who sanctifies (the Shabbat and) the people of Israel and the festivities.

KADESH

On Saturday evening, add:

בָּרוּךְ אַתָּה יְיָ אֱלֹהֵינוּ מֶלֶךְ הָעוֹלָם, בּוֹרֵא מְאוֹרֵי הָאֵשׁ.

Baruch atah Adonai, Eloheinu melech ha-olam, borei me'orei ha-esh.

Blessed are You, Lord our G-d, King of the universe, creator of the light of fire.

בָּרוּךְ אַתָּה יְיָ אֱלֹהֵינוּ מֶלֶךְ הָעוֹלָם הַמַּבְדִּיל בֵּין קֹדֶשׁ לְחֹל, בֵּין אוֹר לְחֹשֶׁךְ, בֵּין יִשְׂרָאֵל לָעַמִּים, בֵּין יוֹם הַשְּׁבִיעִי לְשֵׁשֶׁת יְמֵי הַמַּעֲשֶׂה. בֵּין קְדֻשַּׁת שַׁבָּת לִקְדֻשַּׁת יוֹם טוֹב הִבְדַּלְתָּ, וְאֶת יוֹם הַשְּׁבִיעִי מִשֵּׁשֶׁת יְמֵי הַמַּעֲשֶׂה קִדַּשְׁתָּ. הִבְדַּלְתָּ וְקִדַּשְׁתָּ אֶת עַמְּךָ יִשְׂרָאֵל בִּקְדֻשָּׁתֶךָ. בָּרוּךְ אַתָּה יְיָ הַמַּבְדִּיל בֵּין קֹדֶשׁ לְקֹדֶשׁ.

Baruch atah Adonai, Eloheinu melech ha-olam, ha-mavdil beyn kodesh le-chol, beyn or le-choshech, beyn Israel l'amim, beyn yom ha-shvi'i l'sheshet yemey ha-ma'aseh. Beyn kedushat shabbat l'kedushat yom tov hivdalta, v'et yom ha-shvi'i mi-sheshet yemey ha-ma'aseh kidashta. Hivdalta v'kidashta et amcha Yisrael b'kdushatcha. Baruch atah Adonai ha-mavdil beyn kodesh l'kodesh.

Blessed are You, Lord our G-d, King of the universe, who makes a distinction between the holy and the profane, between light and darkness, between the people of Israel and the nations, between the seventh day and the six days of work. You have made the distinction between the sanctity of Shabbat and the sanctity of the holy day, and sanctified the seventh day of the six days of work. You have set apart and sanctified Your people of Israel with Your holiness. Blessed are You, G-d, who differentiates between the holy and the holy.

On the first Seder night, add:

בָּרוּךְ אַתָּה יְיָ אֱלֹהֵינוּ מֶלֶךְ הָעוֹלָם, שֶׁהֶחֱיָנוּ וְקִיְּמָנוּ וְהִגִּיעָנוּ לַזְּמַן הַזֶּה.

Baruch atah Adonai, Eloheinu melech ha-olam, sh'hecheyanu v'kiyemanu v'higiyanu l'zman hazeh.

Blessed are You, Lord our G-d, King of the universe, who has given us life, sustained us, and allowed us to reach this time.

 Drink the first cup of wine.

URCHATZ וּרְחַץ
Washing Hands

URCHATZ וּרְחַץ

 Wash your hands using a washing cup, pouring water three times onto each hand. Do not recite a blessing.

KARPAS כַּרְפַּס

The Leafy Vegetable

KARPAS כַּרְפַּס

👉 Take some karpas (parsley, celery, or another leafy green vegetable) and dip it into salt water.

📜 Recite the blessing:

בָּרוּךְ אַתָּה יְיָ אֱלֹהֵינוּ מֶלֶךְ הָעוֹלָם, בּוֹרֵא פְּרִי הָאֲדָמָה.

Baruch atah Adonai, Eloheinu Melech ha-olam, borei peri ha-adama.

Blessed are You, Lord our G-d, King of the universe, creator of the fruit of the earth.

👉 After reciting the blessing, eat the karpas.

YACHATZ יַחַץ

Breaking the Middle Matzah

YACHATZ יַחַץ

☞ Of the three matzahs we put aside at the start of the Seder, take the middle one and break it into two. Don't try to break it perfectly in half, as we want to have one piece bigger than the other.

☞ Take the larger piece and set it aside. This will be our Afikoman. It is customary for the leader of the seder to hide the Afikoman during the Seder for younger participants to find.

☞ Return the smaller piece to its place between the first and third matzahs.

MAGID מַגִּיד

Telling the Story of Exodus

מַגִּיד MAGID

   Uncover the Matzah for all to see, and raise it in the air while reciting the following:

הָא לַחְמָא עַנְיָא דִי אֲכָלוּ אַבְהָתָנָא בְּאַרְעָא דְמִצְרָיִם. כָּל דִכְפִין יֵיתֵי וְיֵיכֹל, כָּל דִצְרִיךְ יֵיתֵי וְיִפְסַח. הָשַׁתָּא הָכָא, לְשָׁנָה הַבָּאָה בְּאַרְעָא דְיִשְׂרָאֵל. הָשַׁתָּא עַבְדֵי, לְשָׁנָה הַבָּאָה בְּנֵי חוֹרִין.

Ha lachma anya, di achalu avhatana b'ar'a d'mitsrayim. Kol dichfin yetey v'yechol, kol ditsrich yetey v'yifsach. Hashata hacha, l'shana haba'a b'ara d'yisrael. Hashata avdey, l'shana haba'a bney chorin.

This is the bread of poverty that our ancestors ate in the land of Egypt. All who are hungry may come and eat, all who are in need may come and celebrate with us. Now we are here, here's to next year in the land of Israel. Now we are slaves, here's to next year as a free people.

   Put the matzah down and cover it again.

   Pour the second cup of wine.

MAH NISHTANAH – WHAT IS DIFFERENT?

 It is traditional for the youngest participant of each Seder to ask the four questions, with the rest of the participants replying.

מַה נִּשְׁתַּנָּה הַלַּיְלָה הַזֶּה מִכָּל הַלֵּילוֹת ?

Mah nishtanah halaylah hazeh mikol haleylot?

שֶׁבְּכָל הַלֵּילוֹת אָנוּ אוֹכְלִין חָמֵץ וּמַצָּה, הַלַּיְלָה הַזֶּה - כֻּלּוֹ מַצָּה.

She-b'kol haleylot anu ochlin chametz u'matzah, halaylah hazeh – kulo matzah.

שֶׁבְּכָל הַלֵּילוֹת אָנוּ אוֹכְלִין שְׁאָר יְרָקוֹת, - הַלַּיְלָה הַזֶּה מָרוֹר.

She-b'kol haleylot anu ochlin she'ar yerakot, halaylah hazeh – maror.

שֶׁבְּכָל הַלֵּילוֹת אֵין אָנוּ מַטְבִּילִין אֲפִילוּ פַּעַם אֶחָת, - הַלַּיְלָה הַזֶּה שְׁתֵּי פְעָמִים.

She-b'kol haleylot eyn anu matbilin afilu pa'am achat, halaylah hazeh – shtey pe'amim.

שֶׁבְּכָל הַלֵּילוֹת אָנוּ אוֹכְלִין בֵּין יוֹשְׁבִין וּבֵין מְסֻבִּין, - הַלַּיְלָה הַזֶּה כֻּלָּנוּ מְסֻבִּין.

She-b'kol haleylot anu ochlin beynyoshvin u'beyn mesubin, halaylah hazeh – kulanu mesubin.

What makes this night different from any other night?

On every other night we eat chametz and matzah. On this night – only matzah.

On every other night we eat all kinds of vegetables. On this night – only maror.

On every other night we do not dip our vegetables even once. On this night – we dip twice.

On every other night we eat reclining and sitting straight. On this night – we all recline.

עֲבָדִים הָיִינוּ לְפַרְעֹה בְּמִצְרָיִם, וַיּוֹצִיאֵנוּ יְיָ אֱלֹהֵינוּ מִשָּׁם בְּיָד חֲזָקָה וּבִזְרוֹעַ נְטוּיָה. וְאִלּוּ לֹא הוֹצִיא הַקָּדוֹשׁ בָּרוּךְ הוּא אֶת אֲבוֹתֵינוּ מִמִּצְרַיִם, הֲרֵי אָנוּ וּבָנֵינוּ וּבְנֵי בָנֵינוּ מְשֻׁעְבָּדִים הָיִינוּ לְפַרְעֹה בְּמִצְרָיִם.

Avadim hayinu l'paroh b'mitsrayim, v'yotsi'anu Adonai Eloheinu misham b'yad chazakah u'vizro'a netuya. V'ilu lo hotzi ha-Kadosh Baruch Hu et avoteynu m'mitsrayim, harey anu u'vaneynu u'vney vaneynu meshu'abadim hayinu l'paroh b'mitsrayim

We were slaves of Pharoah in Egypt, until the Lord our G-d took us out from there with a strong hand and an outstretched arm. Had G-d, blessed be His name, not liberated our ancestors from Egypt, we and our sons and daughters and their sons and daughters would still be enslaved to Pharoah in Egypt today.

אֲפִילוּ כֻּלָּנוּ חֲכָמִים, כֻּלָּנוּ נְבוֹנִים, כֻּלָּנוּ זְקֵנִים, כֻּלָּנוּ יוֹדְעִים אֶת הַתּוֹרָה, מִצְוָה עָלֵינוּ לְסַפֵּר בִּיצִיאַת מִצְרָיִם. וְכָל הַמַּרְבֶּה לְסַפֵּר בִּיצִיאַת מִצְרַיִם הֲרֵי זֶה מְשֻׁבָּח.

V'afilu kulanu chachamim, kulanu nevonim, kulanu zkenim, kulanu yod'im et ha-torah, mitzvah aleynu lesaper b'yetsiat mitsrayim. V'chol hamarbeh lesaper b'yetsiat mitsrayim, harey zeh meshubach.

And although we are all intelligent, wise, learned, we all know the torah, we are commanded to tell the story of the Exodus from Egypt. And the more we tell the story, the better.

MAGID

THE FOUR CHILDREN

כְּנֶגֶד אַרְבָּעָה בָנִים דִּבְּרָה תוֹרָה. אֶחָד חָכָם, וְאֶחָד רָשָׁע, וְאֶחָד תָּם, וְאֶחָד שֶׁאֵינוֹ יוֹדֵעַ לִשְׁאוֹל.

Ke-neged arba'ah banim dibrah torah. Echad chacham, v'echad rasha, v'echad tam, v'eched she'eyno yode'a lishol.

The Torah tells us of four children. One who is wise, one who is wicked, one who is simple, and one who does not know how to ask.

23

חָכָם מָה הוּא אוֹמֵר?

מַה הָעֵדוֹת וְהַחֻקִים וְהַמִשְׁפָּטִים אֲשֶׁר צִוָּה יְיָ אֱלֹהֵינוּ אֶתְכֶם?

וְאַף אַתָּה אֱמָר לוֹ כְּהִלְכוֹת הַפֶּסַח: אֵין מַפְטִירִין אַחַר הַפֶּסַח אֲפִיקוֹמָן.

Chacham ma hu omer?

Me ha-edot v'ha-hukim v'ha-mishpatim asher tsivah Adonai Eloheynu etchem?

V'af atah emor lo k'hilchot ha'pesach: eyn maftirin ahar ha-pesach afikoman.

The wise one, what does he say?

"What are these rules and rituals that the Lord our G-d has commanded you?"

And you shall tell him all about the rituals of Passover up until the very last rule, that we do not eat anything else after the Afikoman.

MAGID

רָשָׁע מָה הוּא אוֹמֵר? מָה הָעֲבֹדָה הַזֹּאת לָכֶם? לָכֶם - וְלֹא לוֹ. וּלְפִי שֶׁהוֹצִיא אֶת עַצְמוֹ מִן הַכְּלָל כָּפַר בְּעִקָּר. וְאַף אַתָּה הַקְהֵה אֶת שִׁנָּיו וֶאֱמֹר לוֹ: בַּעֲבוּר זֶה עָשָׂה יְיָ לִי בְּצֵאתִי מִמִּצְרָיִם. לִי - וְלֹא לוֹ. אִילּוּ הָיָה שָׁם, לֹא הָיָה נִגְאָל.

Rasha ma hu omer?
Me ha'avoda hazot lachem? Lachem- v'lo lo. U'lefi she-hotsi et atsmo min ha-klal kafar ba-ikar. V'af atah hakheh et shinav v'emor lo: ba'avur ze asah Adonai li b'tseyti m'mitsrayim. Li- v'lo lo. Ilu hayah sham, lo hayah nigal.

The wicked one, what does he say?

"What are these rules you follow?"

You – and not he. By excluding himself from his people, he denies the foundation of Passover. You shall tell him: It is because of what G-d did for me when I was liberated from Egypt. Me, and not him. Had he been there, he would not have been freed.

תָּם מָה הוּא אוֹמֵר?
מַה זֹּאת?
וְאָמַרְתָּ אֵלָיו: בְּחֹזֶק יָד הוֹצִיאָנוּ יְיָ מִמִּצְרַיִם, מִבֵּית עֲבָדִים.

Tam ma hu omer?
"Ma zot?"
V'amarta eylav: b'chozek yad hotzi'anu Adonai m'mitzrayim, mi-beyt avadim.

The simple one, what does he say?
"What's all this?"
And you shall say to him: G-d liberated us with a mighty hand from Egypt and from slavery.

וְשֶׁאֵינוֹ יוֹדֵעַ לִשְׁאוֹל - אַתְּ פְּתַח לוֹ, שֶׁנֶּאֱמַר: וְהִגַּדְתָּ לְבִנְךָ בַּיּוֹם הַהוּא לֵאמֹר, בַּעֲבוּר זֶה עָשָׂה יְיָ לִי בְּצֵאתִי מִמִּצְרָיִם.

V'she-eyno yode'a lishol – at petach lo, she-ne'emar: v'hi-gadta l'vincha be-yom hahu l'eymor, ba'avur ze asah Adonai li b'tsyeti m'mitsrayim.

And the one who does not know how to ask, you shall tell him the story yourself, as it is said: tell your child on that day, it is because of what G-d did for me when I came out of Egypt.

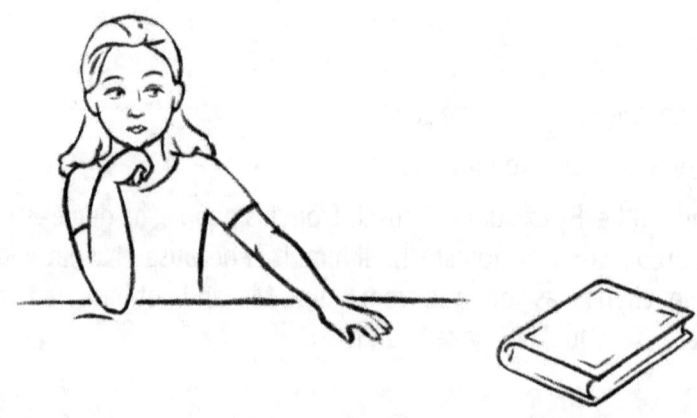

MAGID

 Raise your full cup of wine and say together:

וְהִיא שֶׁעָמְדָה לַאֲבוֹתֵינוּ וְלָנוּ. שֶׁלֹא אֶחָד בִּלְבָד עָמַד עָלֵינוּ לְכַלוֹתֵנוּ, אֶלָא שֶׁבְּכָל דֹוֹר וָדוֹר עוֹמְדִים עָלֵינוּ לְכַלוֹתֵנוּ, וְהַקָדוֹשׁ בָּרוּךְ הוּא מַצִילֵנוּ מִיָדָם.

V'hi she-amda l'avoteynu v'lanu.
She-lo echad bilvad amad aleynu l'chaloteinu, ela she-b'chol dor v'dor, omdim aleynu l'chaloteinu, v'ha-Kadosh Baruch Hu matsileynu m'yadam.

This promise has been upheld for our ancestors and for us.
For over the years, every generation, there have been those who have wanted to defeat and annihilate us, and G-d, Blessed be His Name, has saved us from them time and time again.

 Put down the cup of wine.

THE TEN PLAGUES

אֵלוּ עֶשֶׂר מַכּוֹת שֶׁהֵבִיא הַקָּדוֹשׁ בָּרוּךְ הוּא עַל הַמִּצְרִים בְּמִצְרַיִם, וְאֵלוּ הֵן:

Eylu eser ha-makot she-hevi ha-Kadosh Baruch Hu al ha-mitsrim b'mitsrayim, v'eylu hen:

These are the ten plagues that G-d, Blessed be His Name, brought down upon the Egyptians in Egypt:

 As you recite the ten plagues, pour a drop of wine from your cup onto a plate for each.

דָּם Dam **Blood**

צְפַרְדֵּעַ Tsfardeya **Frogs**

כִּנִּים Kinim **Lice**

עָרוֹב Arov **Wild Beasts**

MAGID

 דֶּבֶר Dever **Plague**

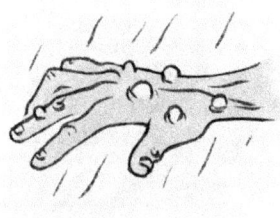 שְׁחִין Shechin **Boils**

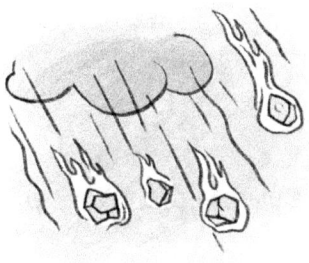 בָּרָד Barad **Hail**

 אַרְבֶּה Arbeh **Locusts**

 חֹשֶׁךְ Choshech **Darkness**

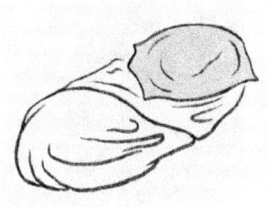 מַכַּת בְּכוֹרוֹת Makat Bechorot **Slaying of the Firstborn**

רַבִּי יְהוּדָה הָיָה נוֹתֵן בָּהֶם סִמָּנִים:

Rabi Yehudah hayah noten ba-hem simanim:

Rabbi Yehuda would assign them mnemonics:

דְּצַ"ךְ	Detsach (blood, frogs, lice)
עֲדַ"שׁ	Adash (wild beasts, plague, boils)
בְּאַחַ"ב	B'achav (hail, locusts, darkness, slaying of the firstborn)

🍷 Pour another drop of wine for each of the three mnemonics.

🍷 Remove the cup of wine and the plate with the wine you spilled and refill your second cup of wine.

DAYEINU

כַּמָּה מַעֲלוֹת טוֹבוֹת לַמָּקוֹם עָלֵינוּ!

אִלּוּ הוֹצִיאָנוּ מִמִּצְרַיִם וְלֹא עָשָׂה בָהֶם שְׁפָטִים, דַּיֵּנוּ.

אִלּוּ עָשָׂה בָהֶם שְׁפָטִים, וְלֹא עָשָׂה בֵאלֹהֵיהֶם, דַּיֵּנוּ.

אִלּוּ עָשָׂה בֵאלֹהֵיהֶם, וְלֹא הָרַג אֶת בְּכוֹרֵיהֶם, דַּיֵּנוּ.

אִלּוּ הָרַג אֶת בְּכוֹרֵיהֶם וְלֹא נָתַן לָנוּ אֶת מָמוֹנָם, דַּיֵּנוּ.

אִלּוּ נָתַן לָנוּ אֶת מָמוֹנָם וְלֹא קָרַע לָנוּ אֶת הַיָּם, דַּיֵּנוּ.

אִלּוּ קָרַע לָנוּ אֶת הַיָּם וְלֹא הֶעֱבִירָנוּ בְתוֹכוֹ בֶּחָרָבָה, דַּיֵּנוּ.

אִלּוּ הֶעֱבִירָנוּ בְתוֹכוֹ בֶּחָרָבָה וְלֹא שִׁקַּע צָרֵנוּ בְּתוֹכוֹ, דַּיֵּנוּ.

אִלּוּ שִׁקַּע צָרֵנוּ בְּתוֹכוֹ וְלֹא סִפֵּק צָרְכֵּנוּ בַּמִּדְבָּר אַרְבָּעִים שָׁנָה, דַּיֵּנוּ.

אִלּוּ סִפֵּק צָרְכֵּנוּ בַּמִּדְבָּר אַרְבָּעִים שָׁנָה וְלֹא הֶאֱכִילָנוּ אֶת הַמָּן, דַּיֵּנוּ.

Kama ma'alot tovot la-makom aleynu!

Ilu hotsi'anu m'mitsrayim v'lo asah vahem shefatim, dayeinu.

Ilu asah behm shefatim v'lo asah b'eloheyhem, dayeinu.

Ilu asah b'eloheyhem v'lo harag et bechoreyhem, dayeinu.

Ilu harag et bechoreyhem v'lo natan lanu et mamonam, dayeinu.

Ilu natan lanu et mamonam v'lo kara lanu et hayam, dayeinu.

Ilu kara lanu et hayam v'lo he'eyviranu betocho b'charavah, dayeinu.

Ilu he'eyviranu betocho b'charavah v'lo shika tsareynu betocho, dayeinu.

Ilu shika tsareynu betocho v'lo sipek tsarcheynu ba-midbar arba'im shanah, dayeinu.

Ilu sipek tsarcheynu ba-midbar arba'im shanah v'lo he'eychilanu et ha-man, dayeinu.

אִלּוּ הֶאֱכִילָנוּ אֶת הַמָּן וְלֹא נָתַן לָנוּ אֶת הַשַּׁבָּת, דַּיֵּינוּ.	Ilu he'eychilanu et ha-man v'lo natan lanu et ha-shabbat, dayeinu.
אִלּוּ קֵרְבָנוּ לִפְנֵי הַר סִינַי, וְלֹא נָתַן לָנוּ אֶת הַתּוֹרָה, דַּיֵּינוּ.	Ilu natan lanu et ha-shabbat v'lo kervanu lifney har sinai, dayeinu.
אִלּוּ נָתַן לָנוּ אֶת הַשַּׁבָּת, וְלֹא קֵרְבָנוּ לִפְנֵי הַר סִינַי, דַּיֵּינוּ.	Ilu kervanu lifney har sinai v'lo natan lanu et ha-torah, dayeinu.
אִלּוּ נָתַן לָנוּ אֶת הַתּוֹרָה וְלֹא הִכְנִיסָנוּ לְאֶרֶץ יִשְׂרָאֵל, דַּיֵּינוּ.	Ilu natan lanu et ha-torah v'lo hichnisanu l'eretz yisrael, dayeinu.
אִלּוּ הִכְנִיסָנוּ לְאֶרֶץ יִשְׂרָאֵל וְלֹא בָנָה לָנוּ אֶת בֵּית הַבְּחִירָה, דַּיֵּינוּ.	Ilu hichnisanu l'eretz Yisrael v'lo vana lanu et beyt ha-behira, dayeinu.

How many good favors G-d has bestowed upon us!

Had He liberated us from Egypt and not carried out justice against the Egyptians, we would have been grateful enough.

Had He carried out justice against the Egyptians and not against their gods, we would have been grateful enough.

Had He carried out justice against their gods and not slain their first-borns, we would have been grateful enough.

Had He slain their firstborns and not given us their treasures, we would have been grateful enough.

Had He given us their treasures and not split the sea for us, we would have been grateful enough.

Had He split the sea for us and not let us through it on dry land, we would have been grateful enough.

Had He led us through the sea on dry land and not drowned our enemies in it, we would have been grateful enough.

Had He drowned our enemies in the sea and not provided for us in the desert for forty years, we would have been grateful enough.

Had He provided for us in the desert for forty years and not given us the manna, we would have been grateful enough.

Had He given us the manna and not given us the Sabbath, we would have been grateful enough.

Had He given us the Sabbath and not brought us to Mount Sinai, we would have been grateful enough.

Had He brought us to Mount Sinai and not given us the Torah, we would have been grateful enough.

Had He given us the Torah and not brought us into Israel, we would have been grateful enough.

Had He brought us into Israel and not built the Temple of worship, we would have been grateful enough.

THE SYMBOLS OF PASSOVER

רַבָּן גַּמְלִיאֵל הָיָה אוֹמֵר: כָּל שֶׁלֹּא אָמַר שְׁלֹשָׁה דְּבָרִים אֵלּוּ בַּפֶּסַח, לֹא יָצָא יְדֵי חוֹבָתוֹ, וְאֵלּוּ הֵן:

Raban Gamilel hayah womer: kol she-lo amar ahloshah devarim eylu ba-pesach, lo yatsa yedey chovato, v'eylu hen:

Rabbi Gamliel would say, all who have not recited these three things on Passover have not done their duty. And these things are:

  All say together:

פֶּסַח, מַצָּה, וּמָרוֹר. Pesach, matzah, u'maror.

Pesach, Matzah, and Bitter Herbs.

MAGID

פֶּסַח שֶׁהָיוּ אֲבוֹתֵינוּ אוֹכְלִים בִּזְמַן שֶׁבֵּית הַמִּקְדָּשׁ הָיָה קַיָּם, עַל שׁוּם מָה?

עַל שׁוּם שֶׁפָּסַח הַקָּדוֹשׁ בָּרוּךְ הוּא עַל בָּתֵּי אֲבוֹתֵינוּ בְּמִצְרַיִם, שֶׁנֶּאֱמַר: וַאֲמַרְתֶּם זֶבַח פֶּסַח הוּא לַיי, אֲשֶׁר פָּסַח עַל בָּתֵּי בְנֵי יִשְׂרָאֵל בְּמִצְרַיִם בְּנָגְפּוֹ אֶת מִצְרַיִם, וְאֶת בָּתֵּינוּ הִצִּיל, וַיִּקֹּד הָעָם וַיִּשְׁתַּחֲווּ.

Pesach she-hayu avoteynu ochlim bizman she-beyt ha-mikdash hayah kayam, al shum mah?

Al shum she-pasach ha-Kadosh Baruch Hu al batey avoteynu b'mitsrayim, she-ne'emar: v'amartem zevach pesach hu l'Adonai, asher pasach al batey bney Yisrael b'mitsrayim b'nogfo et mitsrayim, v'et bateynu hitsil, va-yikod ha'am vayishtachavu.

Pesach, the sacrificial offering that our ancestors would eat while the Temple was standing. What is the meaning of it?

In memory of how G-d passed over the homes of our ancestors in Egypt, sparing them. As it is said: The Pesach is an offering to G-d, who passed over the homes of the Israelites in Egypt as He smote the Egyptians and saved our homes. And the people bowed and genuflected before Him.

Raise the matzah and say:

מַצָּה זוֹ שֶׁאָנוּ אוֹכְלִים, עַל שׁוּם מָה? עַל שׁוּם שֶׁלֹא הִסְפִּיק בְּצֵקָם שֶׁל אֲבוֹתֵינוּ לְהַחֲמִיץ עַד שֶׁנִּגְלָה עֲלֵיהֶם מֶלֶךְ מַלְכֵי הַמְּלָכִים, הַקָּדוֹשׁ בָּרוּךְ הוּא, וּגְאָלָם, שֶׁנֶּאֱמַר: וַיֹּאפוּ אֶת הַבָּצֵק אֲשֶׁר הוֹצִיאוּ מִמִּצְרַיִם עֻגֹת מַצּוֹת, כִּי לֹא חָמֵץ, כִּי גֹרְשׁוּ מִמִּצְרַיִם וְלֹא יָכְלוּ לְהִתְמַהְמֵהַּ, וְגַם צֵדָה לֹא עָשׂוּ לָהֶם.

Matzah zo she-anu ochlim. Al shum mah?
Al shum she-lo hispik betsekam ahel avoteynu l'hachmitz ad she-niglah aleyhem Melech malchei ha-mlachim, Ha-Kadosh Baruch Hu, u'gealam, she-ne'emar: vayofu et ha-batsek asher hotsi'u m'mits-rayim ugot matzot, ki lo cha-metz, ki gorshu m'mitsrayim v'lo yachlu l'hitmahamehah, v'gam tseydah lo asu lahem.

Matzah, this unleavened bread that we eat, what is the meaning of it?
In memory of the unleavened bread that our ancestors made and did not have time to rise before the King of Kings, G-d, Blessed be His Name, appeared before them and redeemed them. It is said: and they baked the dough that they brought with them from Egypt into matzahs, because it did not rise, as they were banished from Egypt and could not delay and did not even have time to prepare provisions.

MAGID

 Raise the maror and say:

מָרוֹר זֶה שֶׁאָנוּ אוֹכְלִים, עַל שׁוּם מָה? עַל שׁוּם שֶׁמֵּרְרוּ הַמִּצְרִים אֶת חַיֵּי אֲבוֹתֵינוּ בְּמִצְרַיִם, שֶׁנֶּאֱמַר: וַיְמָרֲרוּ אֶת חַיֵּיהֶם בַּעֲבֹדָה קָשָׁה, בְּחֹמֶר וּבִלְבֵנִים וּבְכָל עֲבֹדָה בַּשָּׂדֶה אֵת כָּל עֲבֹדָתָם אֲשֶׁר עָבְדוּ בָהֶם בְּפָרֶךְ.

Maror ze she-anu ochlim, al shum mah? Al shum she-mereyru hamitsrim et chayey avoteinu b'mitsrayim, she-ne'emar: vayemareru et chayeyhem b'avoda kasha, b'chomer u'vilvenim u'vechol avoda ba-sadeh et kol avodatam asher avdu baheym b'farech

Maror, these bitter herbs that we eat, what is the meaning of it? In memory of the bitterness that the Egyptians inflicted on the lives of our ancestors. It is said: and they made their lives bitter with hard labor, with mortar and bricks, work in the fields and every form of slavery that they forced upon them.

בְּכָל דּוֹר וָדוֹר חַיָּב אָדָם לִרְאוֹת אֶת עַצְמוֹ כְּאִלּוּ הוּא יָצָא מִמִּצְרַיִם, שֶׁנֶּאֱמַר: וְהִגַּדְתָּ לְבִנְךָ בַּיּוֹם הַהוּא לֵאמֹר, בַּעֲבוּר זֶה עָשָׂה יְיָ לִי בְּצֵאתִי מִמִּצְרָיִם.

B'chol dor va'dor chayav adam lirot et atsmo ke'ilu hu yatsa m'mitsrayim, she-ne'emar: v'higadta l'vincha bayom hahu l'emor: ba'avur ze asah Adonai li b'tseyti m'mitsrayim.

In every generation, every person must see themselves as though they had been liberated from Egypt, as it is said: and on that day, you shall tell your child all that G-d did for you when He set you free from Egypt.

   Drink the second cup of wine, reclining to the left.

RACHTZAH רַחְצָה

Washing Hands
(this time, with a blessing)

רַחְצָה RACHTZAH

☞ Wash your hands again, pouring water from a cup onto each hand three times.

📜 This time, recite the blessing:

בָּרוּךְ אַתָּה יְיָ אֱלֹהֵינוּ מֶלֶךְ הָעוֹלָם, אֲשֶׁר קִדְּשָׁנוּ בְּמִצְוֹתָיו וְצִוָּנוּ עַל נְטִילַת יָדָיִם.

Baruch atah Adonai Eloheinu melech ha-olam, asher kideshanu b'mitzvotav v'tzivanu al netilat yadayim.

Blessed are You, Lord our G-d, King of the universe, who has sanctified us with His commandments and commanded us to wash our hands.

מוֹצִיא מַצָּה
MOTZI-MATZAH

Blessing on the Matzah

מוֹצִיא מַצָּה MOTZI-MATZAH

 Pick up the three matzahs – the two whole ones with the broken half in between them – and raise them in the air.

 Recite the blessing:

בָּרוּךְ אַתָּה יְיָ אֱלֹהֵינוּ מֶלֶךְ הָעוֹלָם הַמּוֹצִיא לֶחֶם מִן הָאָרֶץ.

Baruch atah Adonai Eloheinu melech ha-olam, ha-motzi lechem min ha-aretz.

Blessed are You, Lord our G-d, King of the universe, who produces bread from the earth.

 Now, remove the bottom matzah from the pile and return it to its place. Holding only the top and middle matzahs, recite the following blessing:

בָּרוּךְ אַתָּה יְיָ אֱלֹהֵינוּ מֶלֶךְ הָעוֹלָם, אֲשֶׁר קִדְּשָׁנוּ בְּמִצְוֹתָיו וְצִוָּנוּ עַל אֲכִילַת מַצָּה.

Baruch atah Adonai Eloheinu melech ha-olam, asher kideshanu b'mitzvotav v'tzivanu al achilat matzah.

Blessed are You, Lord our G-d, King of the universe, who has sanctified us with His commandments and commanded us to eat matzah.

 Break off pieces of the top and middle matzahs and distribute them around the table. The matzah should be eaten while reclining to the left.

MAROR מָרוֹר
Bitter Herb

MAROR מָרוֹר

☞ Take a piece of maror (horseradish, lettuce, or another bitter herb) and dip it in the charoset.

📜 Recite the blessing before eating:

בָּרוּךְ אַתָּה יְיָ אֱלֹהֵינוּ מֶלֶךְ הָעוֹלָם, אֲשֶׁר קִדְּשָׁנוּ בְּמִצְוֹתָיו וְצִוָּנוּ עַל אֲכִילַת מָרוֹר.

Baruch atah Adonai Eloheinu melech ha-olam, asher kide-shanu b'mitzvotav v'tzivanu al achilat maror.

Blessed are You, Lord our G-d, King of the universe, who has sanctified us with His commandments and commanded us to eat a bitter herb.

☞ Do not lean while eating the Maror.

KORECH כּוֹרֵךְ

Maror Wrapped in Matzah

KORECH כּוֹרֵךְ

☞ Take two pieces of matzah, put some maror between them, and dip everything in the charoset. You may also spread the charoset on the matzah, add the maror and eat it like a sandwich.

Recite before eating:

זֵכֶר לְמִקְדָּשׁ כְּהִלֵּל. כֵּן עָשָׂה הִלֵּל בִּזְמַן שֶׁבֵּית הַמִּקְדָּשׁ הָיָה קַיָּם: הָיָה כּוֹרֵךְ פֶּסַח מַצָּה וּמָרוֹר וְאוֹכֵל בְּיַחַד, לְקַיֵּם מַה שֶּׁנֶּאֱמַר: עַל מַצּוֹת וּמְרֹרִים יֹאכְלֻהוּ.

Zecher l'mikdash k'hillel. Ken asah hillel bizman she-beyt ha-mikdash hayah kayam. Hayah korech pesach matzah umaror v'ochel beyachad, lekayem mah she-ne'emar: al matzot umerorim yocheluhu.

In memory of the custom of Hillel in the days of the Temple. So Hillel would do while there was a temple: he would wrap the matzah with the maror and eat them together, to observe what is commanded: You shall eat it (the Passover sacrifice) on matzah and maror.

☞ Recline to the left and eat the maror sandwich.

שֻׁלְחָן עוֹרֵךְ
SHULCHAN-ORECH
The Festive Meal

SHULCHAN-ORECH שֻׁלְחָן עוֹרֵךְ:

☞   Now is the time to sit back, relax, and enjoy a delicious festive meal.

☞   At this point, it is customary to eat the hard-boiled egg from the Seder plate, dipped in salt water.

TZAFUN צָפוּן
The Afikoman

TZAFUN צָפוּן

☞ Now that you've finished the meal, it's time to reveal the Afikoman.

☞ If you hid it earlier in the evening, now is the time for whoever found it during the Seder to reveal it.

☞ The Afikoman is the last thing we eat during the Seder night. Break off pieces of the Afikoman matzah and distribute them around the table. Eat the matzah while reclining to your left.

BARECH בָּרֵךְ
Blessing After the Meal

BARECH בָּרֵךְ

 Pour the third cup of wine.

 For the full blessing after the meal, see Birkat Hamazon in the appendix on page 71.

 Recite the blessing on the wine:

בָּרוּךְ אַתָּה יְיָ אֱלֹהֵינוּ מֶלֶךְ הָעוֹלָם בּוֹרֵא פְּרִי הַגָּפֶן.

Baruch atah Adonai Eloheinu melech ha-olam, borei peri ha-gafen.

Blessed are You, Lord our G-d, King of the universe, creator of the fruit of the vine.

 Drink the third cup of wine, while reclining to the left.

 Pour the fourth cup of wine.

 It is customary to pour an extra cup of wine for Elijah the Prophet, who is said to visit on Seder night. Open the front door to invite him in.

Recite the following:

שְׁפֹךְ חֲמָתְךָ אֶל הַגּוֹיִם אֲשֶׁר לֹא יְדָעוּךָ וְעַל מַמְלָכוֹת אֲשֶׁר בְּשִׁמְךָ לֹא קָרָאוּ. כִּי אָכַל אֶת יַעֲקֹב וְאֶת נָוֵהוּ הֵשַׁמּוּ. שְׁפֹךְ עֲלֵיהֶם זַעְמֶךָ וַחֲרוֹן אַפְּךָ יַשִּׂיגֵם. תִּרְדֹּף בְּאַף וְתַשְׁמִידֵם מִתַּחַת שְׁמֵי יְיָ.

Shefoch chamatcha el ha-goy-im asher lo yeda'ucha v'al mamlachot asher b'shimcha lo kar'u. Ki achal et ya'akov v'et navehu heyshamu. Shefoch aleyhem za'amcha v'charon apcha yasigem. Tirdof b'af v'tashmidem mitachat shmey Adonai.

Unleash Your wrath upon the nations who do not acknowledge You and upon the kingdoms who do not call Your Name. For they have devoured Jacob and destroyed his land. Unleash Your fury upon them and let Your anger seize them. Pursue them with rage and destroy them beneath G-d's heavens.

> Some sing Eliyahu Ha'navi, which can be found in the "Songs" section on page 69.

> You may now close the front door.

הַלֵּל HALLEL

Praise to G-d

HALLEL הַלֵּל

　　For the full Hallel, see the Appendix on page 78.

　　Now, make a blessing on the fourth cup of wine:

בָּרוּךְ אַתָּה יְיָ אֱלֹהֵינוּ מֶלֶךְ הָעוֹלָם בּוֹרֵא פְּרִי הַגָּפֶן.

Baruch atah Adonai Eloheinu melech ha-olam, borei peri ha-gafen.

Blessed are You, Lord our G-d, King of the universe, creator of the fruit of the vine.

　　Drink the fourth and final cup of wine while reclining to the left.

　　Recite the final blessing after drinking wine:

בָּרוּךְ אַתָּה יְיָ אֱלֹהֵינוּ מֶלֶךְ הָעוֹלָם, עַל הַגֶּפֶן וְעַל פְּרִי הַגֶּפֶן, עַל תְּנוּבַת הַשָּׂדֶה וְעַל אֶרֶץ חֶמְדָּה טוֹבָה וּרְחָבָה שֶׁרָצִיתָ וְהִנְחַלְתָּ לַאֲבוֹתֵינוּ לֶאֱכֹל מִפִּרְיָהּ וְלִשְׂבֹּעַ מִטּוּבָהּ.

Baruch atah Adonai Eloheinu melech ha-olam, al ha-gefen v'al peri ha-gefen, al tnuvat ha-sadeh v'al eretz chemda tova u'rechava she-ratsita v'hinchalta l'avoteynu le'echol m'pirya v'lisbo'a mituva.

Blessed are You, Lord our G-d, King of the universe, for the vines and the fruit of the vines, for the produce of the field, and for the good, beautiful and vast country which You chose to give to our ancestors so that we may eat from its fruit and be satiated by its goodness.

רַחֵם נָא יְיָ אֱלֹהֵינוּ עַל יִשְׂרָאֵל עַמֶּךָ וְעַל יְרוּשָׁלַיִם עִירֶךָ וְעַל צִיּוֹן מִשְׁכַּן כְּבוֹדֶךָ וְעַל מִזְבְּחֶךָ וְעַל הֵיכָלֶךָ וּבְנֵה יְרוּשָׁלַיִם עִיר הַקֹּדֶשׁ בִּמְהֵרָה בְיָמֵינוּ וְהַעֲלֵנוּ לְתוֹכָהּ וְשַׂמְּחֵנוּ בְּבִנְיָנָהּ וְנֹאכַל מִפִּרְיָהּ וְנִשְׂבַּע מִטּוּבָהּ וּנְבָרֶכְךָ עָלֶיהָ בִּקְדֻשָּׁה וּבְטָהֳרָה.

Rachem na Adonai Eloheinu al Yisrael amcha v'al yerushalayim irecha v'al tsion mishkan kevodecha v'al mizbachecha v'al heichalecha u'vney yerushalayim ir ha-kodesh bimhera b'yameynu v'ha'aleynu l'tochah v'samchenu b'vinyanah v'nochal m'pirya v'nisba mituva u'nevarechecha aleyha b'kdusha uv'tahara.

Please have mercy, Lord our G-d, on Israel Your people, on Jerusalem Your city, on Zion, Your place of rest, on Your altar and Your hall. Rebuild the holy city of Jerusalem in our time and let us ascend to it and be joyous in its grandeur. Then we shall eat from its fruit and be satiated by its goodness and bless You for it with sanctity and purity.

בְּשַׁבָּת: וּרְצֵה וְהַחֲלִיצֵנוּ בְּיוֹם הַשַּׁבָּת הַזֶּה) וְשַׂמְּחֵנוּ בְּיוֹם חַג הַמַּצּוֹת הַזֶּה, כִּי אַתָּה יְיָ טוֹב וּמֵטִיב לַכֹּל וְנוֹדֶה לְּךָ עַל הָאָרֶץ וְעַל פְּרִי הַגָּפֶן.

(on Shabbat: u'retsey v'hachalitseynu b'yom ha-shabbat hazeh) v'samcheynu b'yom chag ha-matzot hazeh, ki atah Adonai tov u'meytiv lakol v'nodeh lecha al ha'aretz v'al peri ha-gafen.

(On Shabbat: Give us strength on this Sabbath day and) let us be happy on this festival of Matzah, because You are good and benevolent to all and we will thank You for the land and for the fruit of the vine.

בָּרוּךְ אַתָּה יְיָ עַל הָאָרֶץ וְעַל פְּרִי הַגָּפֶן.

Baruch ata Adonai, al ha'aretz v'al peri ha-gafen.

Blessed are You, G-d, for the land and for the fruit of the vine.

NIRTZAH נִרְצָה
Conclusion of the Seder

NIRTZAH נִרְצָה

 At the conclusion of the Seder, we celebrate having been able to come together for the festivities and look forward to a prosperous and happy year. Everyone sings together:

לְשָׁנָה הַבָּאָה בִּירוּשָׁלָיִם.   L'shana haba'ah b'Yerushalayim

Next year in Jerusalem!

SONGS
Chad Gadya – One Little Goat

חַד גַּדְיָא, חַד גַּדְיָא, דְּזַבִּין אַבָּא בִּתְרֵי זוּזֵי, חַד גַּדְיָא,חַד גַּדְיָא.

וְאָתָא שׁוּנְרָא וְאָכְלָה לְגַדְיָא, דְּזַבִּין אַבָּא בִּתְרֵי זוּזֵי, חַד גַּדְיָא, חַד גַּדְיָא.

וְאָתָא כַלְבָּא וְנָשַׁךְ לְשׁוּנְרָא, דְּאָכְלָה לְגַדְיָא, דְּזַבִּין אַבָּא בִּתְרֵי זוּזֵי, חַד גַּדְיָא,חַד גַּדְיָא.

וְאָתָא חוּטְרָא וְהִכָּה לְכַלְבָּא, דְּנָשַׁךְ לְשׁוּנְרָא, דְּאָכְלָה לְגַדְיָא, דְּזַבִּין אַבָּא בִּתְרֵי זוּזֵי, חַד גַּדְיָא,חַד גַּדְיָא.

וְאָתָא נוּרָא וְשָׂרַף לְחוּטְרָא, דְּהִכָּה לְכַלְבָּא, דְּנָשַׁךְ לְשׁוּנְרָא, דְּאָכְלָה לְגַדְיָא, דְּזַבִּין אַבָּא בִּתְרֵי זוּזֵי, חַד גַּדְיָא, חַד גַּדְיָא.

וְאָתָא מַיָּא וְכָבָה לְנוּרָא, דְּשָׂרַף לְחוּטְרָא, דְּהִכָּה לְכַלְבָּא, דְּנָשַׁךְ לְשׁוּנְרָא, דְּאָכְלָה לְגַדְיָא, דְּזַבִּין אַבָּא בִּתְרֵי זוּזֵי, חַד גַּדְיָא,חַד גַּדְיָא.

וְאָתָא תוֹרָא וְשָׁתָה לְמַיָּא, דְּכָבָה לְנוּרָא, דְּשָׂרַף לְחוּטְרָא, דְּהִכָּה לְכַלְבָּא, דְּנָשַׁךְ לְשׁוּנְרָא, דְּאָכְלָה לְגַדְיָא, דְּזַבִּין אַבָּא בִּתְרֵי זוּזֵי, חַד גַּדְיָא,חַד גַּדְיָא.

Chad gadya, chad gadya, d'zabin aba b'trei zuzei, chad gadya, chad gadya.

V'ata shunra v'achla l'gadya, d'zabin aba b'trei zuzei, chad gadya, chad gadya.

V'ata chalba v'nashach l'shunra, d'achla l'gadya, d'zabin aba b'trei zuzei, chad gadya, chad gadya.

V'ata chutra v'hica l'calba, d'nashach l'shunra, d'achla l'gadya, d'zabin aba b'trei zuzei, chad gadya, chad gadya.

V'ata nura v'saraf l'chutra, d'hica l'calba, d'nashach l'shunra, d'achla l'gadya, d'zabin aba b'trei zuzei, chad gadya, chad gadya.

V'ata maya v'chaba l'nura, d'saraf l'chutra, d'hica l'calba, d'nashach l'shunra, d'achla l'gadya, d'zabin aba b'trei zuzei, chad gadya, chad gadya.

V'ata tora v'shata l'maya, d'chaba l'nura, d'saraf l'chutra, d'hica l'calba, d'nashach l'shunra, d'achla l'gadya, d'zabin aba b'trei zuzei, chad gadya, chad gadya.

וְאָתָא הַשׁוֹחֵט וְשָׁחַט לְתוֹרָא, דְּשָׁתָה לְמַיָּא, דְּכָבָה לְנוּרָא, דְּשָׂרַף לְחוּטְרָא, דְּהִכָּה לְכַלְבָּא, דְּנָשַׁךְ לְשׁוּנְרָא, דְּאָכְלָה לְגַדְיָא, דְּזַבִּין אַבָּא בִּתְרֵי זוּזֵי, חַד גַּדְיָא, חַד גַּדְיָא.

וְאָתָא מַלְאַךְ הַמָּוֶת וְשָׁחַט לְשׁוֹחֵט, דְּשָׁחַט לְתוֹרָא, דְּשָׁתָה לְמַיָּא, דְּכָבָה לְנוּרָא, דְּשָׂרַף לְחוּטְרָא, דְּהִכָּה לְכַלְבָּא, דְּנָשַׁךְ לְשׁוּנְרָא, דְּאָכְלָה לְגַדְיָא, דְּזַבִּין אַבָּא בִּתְרֵי זוּזֵי, חַד גַּדְיָא, חַד גַּדְיָא.

וְאָתָא הַקָּדוֹשׁ בָּרוּךְ הוּא וְשָׁחַט לְמַלְאַךְ הַמָּוֶת, דְּשָׁחַט לְשׁוֹחֵט, דְּשָׁחַט לְתוֹרָא, דְּשָׁתָה לְמַיָּא, דְּכָבָה לְנוּרָא, דְּשָׂרַף לְחוּטְרָא, דְּהִכָּה לְכַלְבָּא, דְּנָשַׁךְ לְשׁוּנְרָא, דְּאָכְלָה לְגַדְיָא דְּזַבִּין אַבָּא בִּתְרֵי זוּזֵי, חַד גַּדְיָא, חַד גַּדְיָא.

V'ata hashochet v'shachat l'tora, d'shata l'maya, d'chaba l'nura, d'saraf l'chutra, d'hica l'calba, d'nashach l'shunra, d'achla l'gadya, d'zabin aba b'trei zuzei, chad gadya, chad gadya.

V'ata malach hamavet v'shachat l'shochet, d'shachat l'tora, d'shata l'maya, d'chaba l'nura, d'saraf l'chutra, d'hica l'calba, d'nashach l'shunra, d'achla l'gadya, d'zabin aba b'trei zuzei, chad gadya, chad gadya.

V'ata ha-Kadosh Baruch Hu, v'ishachat l'malach hamavet, d'shachat l'shochet, d'shachat l'tora, d'shata l'maya, d'chaba l'nura, d'saraf l'chutra, d'hica l'calba, d'nashach l'shunra, d'achla l'gadya, d'zabin aba b'trei zuzei, chad gadya, chad gadya.

One little goat, one little goat that father bought for two zuzim. One little goat, one little goat.

Along came a cat and ate the goat that father bought for two zuzim. One little goat, one little goat.

Along came a dog and bit the cat that ate the goat that father bought for two zuzim. One little goat, one little goat.

Along came a stick and hit the dog that bit the cat that ate the goat that father bought for two zuzim. One little goat, one little goat.

Along came a fire and burned the stick that hit the dog that bit the cat that ate the goat that father bought for two zuzim. One little goat, one little goat.

Along came some water and put out the fire that burned the stick that hit the dog that bit the cat that ate the goat that father bought for two zuzim. One little goat, one little goat.

Along came an ox and drank the water that put out the fire that burned the stick that hit the dog that bit the cat that ate the goat that father bought for two zuzim. One little goat, one little goat.

Along came a butcher and slaughtered the ox that drank the water that put out the fire that burned the stick that hit the dog that bit the cat that ate the goat that father bought for two zuzim. One little goat, one little goat.

Along came the angel of death and slaughtered the butcher who slaughtered the ox that drank the water that put out the fire that burned the stick that hit the dog that bit the cat that ate the goat that father bought for two zuzim. One little goat, one little goat.

Then along came the Holy One, Blessed be He, and slaughtered the angel of death who slaughtered the butcher who slaughtered the ox that drank the water that put out the fire that burned the stick that hit the dog that bit the cat that ate the goat that father bought for two zuzim. One little goat, one little goat.

Echad Mi Yodeya – Who Knows One?

אֶחָד מִי יוֹדֵעַ? אֶחָד אֲנִי יוֹדֵעַ. אֶחָד אֱלֹהֵינוּ שֶׁבַּשָּׁמַיִם וּבָאָרֶץ.

Echad mi yodea? Echad ani yodea. Echad Eloheinu she-bashamayim u'va'aretz.

שְׁנַיִם מִי יוֹדֵעַ? שְׁנַיִם אֲנִי יוֹדֵעַ. שְׁנֵי לוּחוֹת הַבְּרִית, אֶחָד אֱלֹהֵינוּ שֶׁבַּשָּׁמַיִם וּבָאָרֶץ.

Shnayim mi yodea? Shnayim ani yodea. Shnei luchot ha-brit, echad Eloheinu she-bashamayim u'va'aretz.

שְׁלֹשָׁה מִי יוֹדֵעַ? שְׁלֹשָׁה אֲנִי יוֹדֵעַ. שְׁלֹשָׁה אָבוֹת, שְׁנֵי לוּחוֹת הַבְּרִית, אֶחָד אֱלֹהֵינוּ שֶׁבַּשָּׁמַיִם וּבָאָרֶץ.

Shloshah mi yodea? Shloshah ani yodea. Shloshah avot, shnei luchot ha-brit, echad Eloheinu she-bashamayim u'va'aretz.

אַרְבַּע מִי יוֹדֵעַ? אַרְבַּע אֲנִי יוֹדֵעַ. אַרְבַּע אִמָּהוֹת, שְׁלֹשָׁה אָבוֹת, שְׁנֵי לוּחוֹת הַבְּרִית, אֶחָד אֱלֹהֵינוּ שֶׁבַּשָּׁמַיִם וּבָאָרֶץ.

Arbah mi yodea? Arbah ani yodea. Arbah imahot, shloshah avot, shnei luchot ha-brit, echad Eloheinu she-bashamayim u'va'aretz.

חֲמִשָּׁה מִי יוֹדֵעַ? חֲמִשָּׁה אֲנִי יוֹדֵעַ. חֲמִשָּׁה חֻמְשֵׁי תוֹרָה, אַרְבַּע אִמָּהוֹת, שְׁלֹשָׁה אָבוֹת, שְׁנֵי לוּחוֹת הַבְּרִית, אֶחָד אֱלֹהֵינוּ שֶׁבַּשָּׁמַיִם וּבָאָרֶץ.

Chamishah mi yodea? Chamishah ani yodea. Chamishah chumshei Torah, arbah imahot, shloshah avot, shnei luchot ha-brit, echad Eloheinu she-bashamayim u'va'aretz.

שִׁשָּׁה מִי יוֹדֵעַ? שִׁשָּׁה אֲנִי יוֹדֵעַ. שִׁשָּׁה סִדְרֵי מִשְׁנָה, חֲמִשָּׁה חֻמְשֵׁי תוֹרָה, אַרְבַּע אִמָּהוֹת, שְׁלֹשָׁה אָבוֹת שְׁנֵי לוּחוֹת הַבְּרִית, אֶחָד אֱלֹהֵינוּ שֶׁבַּשָּׁמַיִם וּבָאָרֶץ.

Shishah mi yodea? Shishah ani yodea. Shishah sidrei mishnah, chamishah chumshei Torah, arbah imahot, shloshah avot, shnei luchot ha-brit, echad Eloheinu she-bashamayim u'va'aretz.

SONGS

שִׁבְעָה מִי יוֹדֵעַ? שִׁבְעָה אֲנִי יוֹדֵעַ. שִׁבְעָה יְמֵי שַׁבְּתָא, שִׁשָּׁה סִדְרֵי מִשְׁנָה, חֲמִשָּׁה חֻמְשֵׁי תוֹרָה, אַרְבַּע אִמָּהוֹת, שְׁלֹשָׁה אָבוֹת, שְׁנֵי לוּחוֹת הַבְּרִית, אֶחָד אֱלֹהֵינוּ שֶׁבַּשָּׁמַיִם וּבָאָרֶץ.

שְׁמוֹנָה מִי יוֹדֵעַ? שְׁמוֹנָה אֲנִי יוֹדֵעַ. שְׁמוֹנָה יְמֵי מִילָה, שִׁבְעָה יְמֵי שַׁבְּתָא, שִׁשָּׁה סִדְרֵי מִשְׁנָה, חֲמִשָּׁה חֻמְשֵׁי תוֹרָה, אַרְבַּע אִמָּהוֹת, שְׁלֹשָׁה אָבוֹת, שְׁנֵי לוּחוֹת הַבְּרִית, אֶחָד אֱלֹהֵינוּ שֶׁבַּשָּׁמַיִם וּבָאָרֶץ.

תִּשְׁעָה מִי יוֹדֵעַ? תִּשְׁעָה אֲנִי יוֹדֵעַ. תִּשְׁעָה יַרְחֵי לֵדָה, שְׁמוֹנָה יְמֵי מִילָה, שִׁבְעָה יְמֵי שַׁבְּתָא, שִׁשָּׁה סִדְרֵי מִשְׁנָה, חֲמִשָּׁה חֻמְשֵׁי תוֹרָה, אַרְבַּע אִמָּהוֹת, שְׁלֹשָׁה אָבוֹת, שְׁנֵי לוּחוֹת הַבְּרִית, אֶחָד אֱלֹהֵינוּ שֶׁבַּשָּׁמַיִם וּבָאָרֶץ.

עֲשָׂרָה מִי יוֹדֵעַ? עֲשָׂרָה אֲנִי יוֹדֵעַ. עֲשָׂרָה דִבְּרַיָּא, תִּשְׁעָה יַרְחֵי לֵדָה, שְׁמוֹנָה יְמֵי מִילָה, שִׁבְעָה יְמֵי שַׁבְּתָא, שִׁשָּׁה סִדְרֵי מִשְׁנָה, חֲמִשָּׁה חֻמְשֵׁי תוֹרָה, אַרְבַּע אִמָּהוֹת, שְׁלֹשָׁה אָבוֹת, שְׁנֵי לוּחוֹת הַבְּרִית, אֶחָד אֱלֹהֵינוּ שֶׁבַּשָּׁמַיִם וּבָאָרֶץ.

Shivah mi yodea? Shivah ani yodea. Shivah y'mei shabtah, shishah sidrei mishnah, chamishah chumshei Torah, arbah imahot, shloshah avot, shnei luchot ha-brit, echad Eloheinu she-bashamayim u'va'aretz.

Shmonah mi yodea? Shmonah ani yodea. Shmonah y'mei milah, shivah y'mei shabtah, shishah sidrei mishnah, chamishah chumshei Torah, arbah imahot, shloshah avot, shnei luchot ha-brit, echad Eloheinu she-bashamayim u'va'aretz.

Tishah mi yodea? Tishah ani yodea. Tishah yarchei leidah, shmonah y'mei milah, shivah y'mei shabtah, shishah sidrei mishnah, chamishah chumshei Torah, arbah imahot, shloshah avot, shnei luchot ha-brit, echad Eloheinu she-bashamayim u'va'aretz.

Asarah mi yodea? Asarah ani yodea. Asarah dibrayah, tishah yarchei leidah, shmonah y'mei milah, shivah y'mei shabtah, shishah sidrei mishnah, chamishah chumshei Torah, arbah imahot, shloshah avot, shnei luchot ha-brit, echad Eloheinu she-bashamayim u'va'aretz.

אַחַד עָשָׂר מִי יוֹדֵעַ? אַחַד עָשָׂר אֲנִי יוֹדֵעַ. אַחַד עָשָׂר כּוֹכְבַיָּא, עֲשָׂרָה דִבְּרַיָּא, תִּשְׁעָה יַרְחֵי לֵדָה, שְׁמוֹנָה יְמֵי מִילָה, שִׁבְעָה יְמֵי שַׁבַּתָּא, שִׁשָּׁה סִדְרֵי מִשְׁנָה, חֲמִשָּׁה חֻמְשֵׁי תוֹרָה, אַרְבַּע אִמָּהוֹת, שְׁלֹשָׁה אָבוֹת, שְׁנֵי לוּחוֹת הַבְּרִית, אֶחָד אֱלֹהֵינוּ שֶׁבַּשָּׁמַיִם וּבָאָרֶץ.

שְׁנֵים עָשָׂר מִי יוֹדֵעַ? שְׁנֵים עָשָׂר אֲנִי יוֹדֵעַ. שְׁנֵים עָשָׂר שִׁבְטַיָּא, אַחַד עָשָׂר כּוֹכְבַיָּא, עֲשָׂרָה דִבְּרַיָּא, תִּשְׁעָה יַרְחֵי לֵדָה, שְׁמוֹנָה יְמֵי מִילָה, שִׁבְעָה יְמֵי שַׁבַּתָּא, שִׁשָּׁה סִדְרֵי מִשְׁנָה, חֲמִשָּׁה חֻמְשֵׁי תוֹרָה, אַרְבַּע אִמָּהוֹת, שְׁלֹשָׁה אָבוֹת, שְׁנֵי לוּחוֹת הַבְּרִית, אֶחָד אֱלֹהֵינוּ שֶׁבַּשָּׁמַיִם וּבָאָרֶץ.

שְׁלֹשָׁה עָשָׂר מִי יוֹדֵעַ? שְׁלֹשָׁה עָשָׂר אֲנִי יוֹדֵעַ. שְׁלֹשָׁה עָשָׂר מִדַּיָּא, שְׁנֵים עָשָׂר שִׁבְטַיָּא, אַחַד עָשָׂר כּוֹכְבַיָּא, עֲשָׂרָה דִבְּרַיָּא, תִּשְׁעָה יַרְחֵי לֵדָה, שְׁמוֹנָה יְמֵי מִילָה, שִׁבְעָה יְמֵי שַׁבַּתָּא, שִׁשָּׁה סִדְרֵי מִשְׁנָה, חֲמִשָּׁה חֻמְשֵׁי תוֹרָה, אַרְבַּע אִמָּהוֹת, שְׁלֹשָׁה אָבוֹת, שְׁנֵי לוּחוֹת הַבְּרִית, אֶחָד אֱלֹהֵינוּ שֶׁבַּשָּׁמַיִם וּבָאָרֶץ.

Achad-asar mi yodea? Achad-asar ani yodea. Achad-asar kochvayah, asarah dibrayah, tishah yarchei leidah, shmonah y'mei milah, shivah y'mei shabtah, shishah sidrei mishnah, chamishah chumshei Torah, arbah imahot, shloshah avot, shnei luchot ha-brit, echad Eloheinu she-bashamayim u'va'aretz.

Shneim-asar mi yodea? Shneim-asar ani yodea. Shneim-asar shivtayah, achad-asar kochvayah, asarah dibrayah, tishah yarchei leidah, shmonah y'mei milah, shivah y'mei shabtah, shishah sidrei mishnah, chamishah chumshei Torah, arbah imahot, shloshah avot, shnei luchot ha-brit, echad Eloheinu she-bashamayim u'va'aretz.

Shloshah-asar mi yodea? Shloshah-asar ani yodea. Shloshah-asar midayah, shneim-asar shivtayah, achad-asar kochvayah, asarah dibrayah, tishah yarchei leidah, shmonah y'mei milah, shivah y'mei shabtah, shishah sidrei mishnah, chamishah chumshei Torah, arbah imahot, shloshah avot, shnei luchot ha-brit, echad Eloheinu she-bashamayim u'va'aretz.

Who knows one? I know one. One is our G-d in Heaven and Earth.

Who knows two? I know two. Two are the tablets of the covenant. One is our G-d in Heaven and Earth.

Who knows three? I know three. Three are the patriarchs. Two are the tablets of the covenant. One is our G-d in Heaven and Earth.

Who knows four? I know four. Four are the matriarchs. Three are the patriarchs. Two are the tablets of the covenant. One is our G-d in Heaven and Earth.

Who knows five? I know five. Five are the books of the Torah. Four are the matriarchs. Three are the patriarchs. Two are the tablets of the covenant. One is our G-d in Heaven and Earth.

Who knows six? I know six. Six are the orders of the Mishnah. Five are the books of the Torah. Four are the matriarchs. Three are the patriarchs. Two are the tablets of the covenant. One is our G-d in Heaven and Earth.

Who knows seven? I know seven. Seven are the days of the week. Six are the orders of the Mishnah. Five are the books of the Torah. Four are the matriarchs. Three are the patriarchs. Two are the tablets of the covenant. One is our G-d in Heaven and Earth

Who knows eight? I know eight. Eight are the days for circumcision. Seven are the days of the week. Six are the orders of the Mishnah. Five are the books of the Torah. Four are the matriarchs. Three are the patriarchs. Two are the tablets of the covenant. One is our G-d in Heaven and Earth.

Who knows nine? I know nine. Nine are the months of childbirth. Eight are the days for circumcision. Seven are the days of the week. Six are the orders of the Mishnah. Five are the books of the Torah. Four are the matriarchs. Three are the patriarchs. Two are the tablets of the covenant. One is our G-d in Heaven and Earth.

Who knows ten? I know ten. Ten are the Words from Sinai. Nine are the months of childbirth. Eight are the days for circumcision. Seven are the days of the week. Six are the orders of the Mishnah. Five are the books of the Torah. Four are the matriarchs. Three are the patriarchs. Two are the tablets of the covenant. One is our G-d in Heaven and Earth.

Who knows eleven? I know eleven. Eleven are the stars. Ten are the Words from Sinai. Nine are the months of childbirth. Eight are the days for circumcision. Seven are the days of the week. Six are the orders of the Mishnah. Five are the books of the Torah. Four are the matriarchs. Three are the patriarchs. Two are the tablets of the covenant. One is our G-d in Heaven and Earth.

Who knows twelve? I know twelve. Twelve are the tribes. Eleven are the stars. Ten are the Words from Sinai. Nine are the months of childbirth. Eight are the days for circumcision. Seven are the days of the week. Six are the orders of the Mishnah. Five are the books of the Torah. Four are the matriarchs. Three are the patriarchs. Two are the tablets of the covenant. One is our G-d in Heaven and Earth.

Who knows thirteen? I know thirteen. Thirteen are the attributes of G-d. Twelve are the tribes. Eleven are the stars. Ten are the Words from Sinai. Nine are the months of childbirth. Eight are the days for circumcision. Seven are the days of the week. Six are the orders of the Mishnah. Five are the books of the Torah. Four are the matriarchs. Three are the patriarchs. Two are the tablets of the covenant. One is our G-d in Heaven and Earth.

Eliyahu Hanavi – The Prophet Elijah

אֵלִיָהוּ הַנָבִיא, אֵלִיָהוּ הַתִשְׁבִּי,
אֵלִיָהוּ הַגִלְעָדִי, בִּמְהֵרָה יָבֹא
אֵלֵינוּ עִם מָשִׁיחַ בֶּן דָוִד.

Eliyahu ha-navi, Eliyahu ha-tishbi, Eliyahu ha-giladi. Bimheirah yavo eleynu, im Mashiach ben David.

May Elijah the prophet, Elijah the Tishbite, Elijah of Gilead, quickly in our day come to us heralding redemption with the Messiah, son of David.

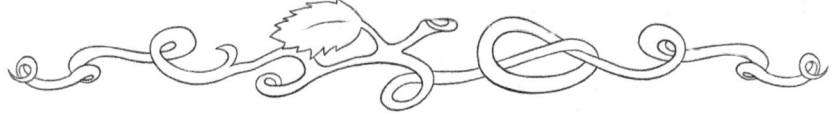

Let My People Go

"When Israel was in Egypt land, let my people go.
Oppressed so hard they could not stand, let my people go."
Go down, Moses, way down in Egypt land.
Tell old Pharaoh, let my people go!

"Thus saith the Lord" bold Moses said, "Let my people go,
If not I'll smite your firstborn dead, let my people go."
Go down, Moses, way down in Egypt land.
Tell old Pharaoh, let my people go!

"No more shall they in bondage toil, let my people go.
Let them come out with Egypt's spoils, let my people go."
Go down, Moses, way down in Egypt land.
Tell old Pharaoh, let my people go!

"When people stop this slavery, let my people go.
Soon may all the earth be free, let my people go."
Go down, Moses, way down in Egypt land.
Tell old Pharaoh, let my people go!

APPENDIX – ADDITIONS
Birkat Hamazon – Grace after the Meal

שִׁיר הַמַּעֲלוֹת בְּשׁוּב יְיָ אֶת שִׁיבַת צִיּוֹן הָיִינוּ כְּחֹלְמִים. אָז יִמָּלֵא שְׂחוֹק פִּינוּ וּלְשׁוֹנֵנוּ רִנָּה אָז יֹאמְרוּ בַגּוֹיִם הִגְדִּיל יְיָ לַעֲשׂוֹת עִם אֵלֶּה. הִגְדִּיל יְיָ לַעֲשׂוֹת עִמָּנוּ הָיִינוּ שְׂמֵחִים. שׁוּבָה יְיָ אֶת שְׁבִיתֵנוּ כַּאֲפִיקִים בַּנֶּגֶב. הַזֹּרְעִים בְּדִמְעָה בְּרִנָּה יִקְצֹרוּ. הָלוֹךְ יֵלֵךְ וּבָכֹה נֹשֵׂא מֶשֶׁךְ הַזָּרַע בֹּא יָבוֹא בְרִנָּה נֹשֵׂא אֲלֻמֹּתָיו.

The song of virtues — when the Lord returned the captives of Zion, we were like people in a dream. Then our mouth filled with laughter, and our tongue with joy: and they said among the nations, The Lord has done great things for them. The Lord has done great things for us, so we rejoice. Bring back our captives, G-d, like the rivers that flow in the south. They who sow in tears shall reap in joy. Though he goes on his way weeping, bearing the store of seed, he shall come back with joy, bearing his sheaves.

בָּרוּךְ אַתָּה יְיָ אֱלֹהֵינוּ מֶלֶךְ הָעוֹלָם, הַזָּן אֶת הָעוֹלָם כֻּלּוֹ בְּטוּבוֹ בְּחֵן בְּחֶסֶד וּבְרַחֲמִים, הוּא נֹתֵן לֶחֶם לְכָל-בָּשָׂר כִּי לְעוֹלָם חַסְדּוֹ, וּבְטוּבוֹ הַגָּדוֹל תָּמִיד לֹא חָסַר לָנוּ וְאַל יֶחְסַר לָנוּ מָזוֹן לְעוֹלָם וָעֶד, בַּעֲבוּר שְׁמוֹ הַגָּדוֹל, כִּי הוּא אֵל זָן וּמְפַרְנֵס לַכֹּל, וּמֵטִיב לַכֹּל וּמֵכִין מָזוֹן לְכָל-בְּרִיּוֹתָיו אֲשֶׁר בָּרָא. בָּרוּךְ אַתָּה יְיָ הַזָּן אֶת הַכֹּל.

Blessed are You, Lord our G-d, King of the universe, who benevolently provides for the whole world with grace, charity, and mercy. He gives bread to all who live, and His charity is never-ending. Thanks to His goodness we never lack and never will lack for food as long as we live, because His name is great and He feeds and sustains us all and provides nourishment to all the creatures He created. Blessed are You, G-d, who provides food for all.

נוֹדֶה לְךָ יְיָ אֱלֹהֵינוּ עַל שֶׁהִנְחַלְתָּ לַאֲבוֹתֵינוּ אֶרֶץ חֶמְדָּה טוֹבָה וּרְחָבָה, וְעַל שֶׁהוֹצֵאתָנוּ יְיָ אֱלֹהֵינוּ מֵאֶרֶץ מִצְרַיִם וּפְדִיתָנוּ מִבֵּית עֲבָדִים, וְעַל בְּרִיתְךָ שֶׁחָתַמְתָּ בִּבְשָׂרֵנוּ וְעַל תּוֹרָתְךָ שֶׁלִּמַּדְתָּנוּ וְעַל חֻקֶּיךָ שֶׁהוֹדַעְתָּנוּ, וְעַל חַיִּים חֵן וָחֶסֶד שֶׁחוֹנַנְתָּנוּ, וְעַל אֲכִילַת מָזוֹן שָׁאַתָּה זָן וּמְפַרְנֵס אוֹתָנוּ תָּמִיד, בְּכָל יוֹם וּבְכָל עֵת וּבְכָל שָׁעָה.

We thank You, Lord our G-d, for bequeathing our ancestors a good and spacious land, and for liberating us from the land of Egypt and saving us from slavery. We thank You also for the covenant You have marked on our skin, the Torah You have taught us, the rules You have given us, the life of grace and mercy You have blessed us with, and the food You provide us always, every day, every moment, and every hour.

וְעַל הַכֹּל יְיָ אֱלֹהֵינוּ אֲנַחְנוּ מוֹדִים לָךְ וּמְבָרְכִים אוֹתָךְ, יִתְבָּרַךְ שִׁמְךָ בְּפִי כָּל חַי תָּמִיד לְעוֹלָם וָעֶד, כַּכָּתוּב: "וְאָכַלְתָּ וְשָׂבָעְתָּ, וּבֵרַכְתָּ אֶת יְיָ אֱלֹהֶיךָ עַל הָאָרֶץ הַטּוֹבָה אֲשֶׁר נָתַן לָךְ". בָּרוּךְ אַתָּה יְיָ, עַל הָאָרֶץ וְעַל הַמָּזוֹן.

For all this, Lord our G-d, we thank You and bless You, may Your name be blessed by every living being always. As it is said: "and You shall eat and be satisfied and thank G-d for the good land he has given You." Blessed are You, G-d, for the land and for the food.

רַחֵם נָא יְיָ אֱלֹהֵינוּ עַל יִשְׂרָאֵל עַמֶּךָ, וְעַל יְרוּשָׁלַיִם עִירֶךָ, וְעַל צִיּוֹן מִשְׁכַּן כְּבוֹדֶךָ, וְעַל מַלְכוּת בֵּית דָּוִד מְשִׁיחֶךָ, וְעַל הַבַּיִת הַגָּדוֹל וְהַקָּדוֹשׁ שֶׁנִּקְרָא שִׁמְךָ עָלָיו. אֱלֹהֵינוּ, אָבִינוּ,

רְעֵנוּ, זוּנֵנוּ, פַּרְנְסֵנוּ וְכַלְכְּלֵנוּ וְהַרְוִיחֵנוּ, וְהַרְוַח לָנוּ יְיָ אֱלֹהֵינוּ מְהֵרָה מִכָּל צָרוֹתֵינוּ. וְנָא אַל תַּצְרִיכֵנוּ יְיָ אֱלֹהֵינוּ, לֹא לִידֵי מַתְּנַת בָּשָׂר וָדָם וְלֹא לִידֵי הַלְוָאָתָם, כִּי אִם לְיָדְךָ הַמְּלֵאָה הַפְּתוּחָה הַקְּדוֹשָׁה וְהָרְחָבָה, שֶׁלֹּא נֵבוֹשׁ וְלֹא נִכָּלֵם לְעוֹלָם וָעֶד.

Please have mercy, Lord our G-d, on Israel Your people, on Jerusalem Your city, on Zion, Your place of rest, on the kingdom of the house of David Your Messiah, and on the great and holy Temple called by Your name. Our G-d, our father, our friend, our provider, sustain us, feed us, and nourish us; and grant us, Lord our G-d, relief from our woes. Please do not let us be dependent on gifts or loans of flesh and blood, but only upon Your full, open, generous, and holy hand; let us not be shamed or disgraced ever again.

☞ Add on Shabbat:

(**הַצֵּר** וְהַחֲלִיצֵנוּ יְיָ אֱלֹהֵינוּ בְּמִצְוֹתֶיךָ וּבְמִצְוַת יוֹם הַשְּׁבִיעִי הַשַּׁבָּת הַגָּדוֹל וְהַקָּדוֹשׁ הַזֶּה. כִּי יוֹם זֶה גָּדוֹל וְקָדוֹשׁ הוּא לְפָנֶיךָ לִשְׁבָּת בּוֹ וְלָנוּחַ בּוֹ בְּאַהֲבָה כְּמִצְוַת רְצוֹנֶךָ. וּבִרְצוֹנְךָ הָנִיחַ לָנוּ יְיָ אֱלֹהֵינוּ שֶׁלֹּא תְהֵא צָרָה וְיָגוֹן וַאֲנָחָה בְּיוֹם מְנוּחָתֵנוּ. וְהַרְאֵנוּ יְיָ אֱלֹהֵינוּ בְּנֶחָמַת צִיּוֹן עִירֶךָ וּבְבִנְיַן יְרוּשָׁלַיִם עִיר קָדְשֶׁךָ כִּי אַתָּה הוּא בַּעַל הַיְשׁוּעוֹת וּבַעַל הַנֶּחָמוֹת.)

(If it please You, Lord our G-d, give us strength through Your commandments and the commandment of the seventh day, this great and holy Shabbat. For this day is great and holy to You, a day to rest and refrain with love, as You have commanded. Please let us have peace, Lord our G-d, so that no troubles will afflict us on our day of rest. Let us see the return of Zion Your city and the rebuilding of Jerusalem Your holy city, for You are master of redemption and comfort.)

אֱלֹהֵינוּ וֵאלֹהֵי אֲבוֹתֵינוּ, יַעֲלֶה וְיָבֹא וְיַגִּיעַ, וְיֵרָאֶה וְיֵרָצֶה וְיִשָּׁמַע, וְיִפָּקֵד וְיִזָּכֵר זִכְרוֹנֵנוּ וּפִקְדוֹנֵנוּ וְזִכְרוֹן אֲבוֹתֵינוּ, וְזִכְרוֹן מָשִׁיחַ בֶּן דָּוִד עַבְדֶּךָ, וְזִכְרוֹן יְרוּשָׁלַיִם עִיר קָדְשֶׁךָ, וְזִכְרוֹן כָּל עַמְּךָ בֵּית יִשְׂרָאֵל לְפָנֶיךָ לִפְלֵטָה, לְטוֹבָה, לְחֵן וּלְחֶסֶד וּלְרַחֲמִים, לְחַיִּים וּלְשָׁלוֹם, בְּיוֹם חַג הַמַּצּוֹת הַזֶּה.

זָכְרֵנוּ יְיָ אֱלֹהֵינוּ בּוֹ לְטוֹבָה, וּפָקְדֵנוּ בוֹ לִבְרָכָה, וְהוֹשִׁיעֵנוּ בוֹ לְחַיִּים נוסח ספרד: טוֹבִים; וּבִדְבַר יְשׁוּעָה וְרַחֲמִים חוּס וְחָנֵּנוּ, וְרַחֵם עָלֵינוּ וְהוֹשִׁיעֵנוּ, כִּי אֵלֶיךָ עֵינֵינוּ, כִּי אֵל מֶלֶךְ חַנּוּן וְרַחוּם אָתָּה.

Our G-d and the G-d of our ancestors, may our memory, the memory of our ancestors, the memory of the Messiah son of David Your servant, the memory of Jerusalem Your holy city, and the memory of the people of Israel rise and come and be seen and accepted and heard and considered in goodness, grace, charity, mercy, life, and peace, on this festival of matzah.

Remember us kindly, Lord our G-d, consider us with Your blessing, and redeem us to a good life. With the promise of salvation and mercy, spare us and save us, for our eyes look to You, for You are a king of mercy and compassion.

וּבְנֵה יְרוּשָׁלַיִם עִיר הַקֹּדֶשׁ בִּמְהֵרָה בְיָמֵינוּ. בָּרוּךְ אַתָּה יְיָ, בּוֹנֵה בְרַחֲמָיו יְרוּשָׁלָיִם.

May You rebuild Your holy city of Jerusalem in our time. Blessed are you, G-d, who rebuilds Jerusalem in His mercy.

בָּרוּךְ אַתָּה יְיָ, אֱלֹהֵינוּ מֶלֶךְ הָעוֹלָם, הָאֵל אָבִינוּ, מַלְכֵּנוּ, אַדִּירֵנוּ, בּוֹרְאֵנוּ, גֹּאֲלֵנוּ, יוֹצְרֵנוּ, קְדוֹשֵׁנוּ קְדוֹשׁ יַעֲקֹב, רוֹעֵנוּ

ADDITIONS

רוֹעֵה יִשְׂרָאֵל, הַמֶּלֶךְ הַטּוֹב וְהַמֵּטִיב לַכֹּל, שֶׁבְּכָל יוֹם וָיוֹם הוּא הֵטִיב, הוּא מֵטִיב, הוּא יֵיטִיב לָנוּ. הוּא גְמָלָנוּ הוּא גוֹמְלֵנוּ הוּא יִגְמְלֵנוּ לָעַד, לְחֵן וּלְחֶסֶד וּלְרַחֲמִים וּלְרֶוַח הַצָּלָה וְהַצְלָחָה, בְּרָכָה וִישׁוּעָה נֶחָמָה פַּרְנָסָה וְכַלְכָּלָה, וְרַחֲמִים וְחַיִּים וְשָׁלוֹם וְכָל טוֹב; וּמִכָּל טוּב לְעוֹלָם עַל יְחַסְּרֵנוּ.

Blessed are You, Lord our G-d, King of the universe, the Lord of our fathers, our king, our master, our creator, our savior, our maker, our holy one and Jacob's holy one, our shepherd and the shepherd of Israel, the kind and benevolent king, who showers us with good every day past, present, and future. He sentences us in the past, present, and future, to grace and charity and mercy and wellbeing and redemption and success, blessing and salvation and comfort and sustenance and livelihood and mercy and good life and all that is good; may we never want for anything ever.

הָרַחֲמָן הוּא יִמְלוֹךְ עָלֵינוּ לְעוֹלָם וָעֶד.
הָרַחֲמָן הוּא יִתְבָּרַךְ בַּשָּׁמַיִם וּבָאָרֶץ.
הָרַחֲמָן הוּא יִשְׁתַּבַּח לְדוֹר דּוֹרִים, וְיִתְפָּאַר בָּנוּ לָעַד וּלְנֵצַח נְצָחִים, וְיִתְהַדַּר בָּנוּ לָעַד וּלְעוֹלְמֵי עוֹלָמִים.
הָרַחֲמָן הוּא יְפַרְנְסֵנוּ בְּכָבוֹד.
הָרַחֲמָן הוּא יִשְׁבּוֹר עֻלֵּנוּ מֵעַל צַוָּארֵנוּ, וְהוּא יוֹלִיכֵנוּ קוֹמְמִיּוּת לְאַרְצֵנוּ.
הָרַחֲמָן הוּא יִשְׁלַח לָנוּ בְּרָכָה מְרֻבָּה בַּבַּיִת הַזֶּה, וְעַל שֻׁלְחָן זֶה שֶׁאָכַלְנוּ עָלָיו.
הָרַחֲמָן הוּא יִשְׁלַח לָנוּ אֶת אֵלִיָּהוּ הַנָּבִיא זָכוּר לַטּוֹב, וִיבַשֶּׂר לָנוּ בְּשׂוֹרוֹת טוֹבוֹת יְשׁוּעוֹת וְנֶחָמוֹת.
(הָרַחֲמָן הוּא יַנְחִילֵנוּ יוֹם שֶׁכֻּלּוֹ שַׁבָּת וּמְנוּחָה לְחַיֵּי הָעוֹלָמִים.)
הָרַחֲמָן הוּא יַנְחִילֵנוּ יוֹם שֶׁכֻּלּוֹ טוֹב.
הָרַחֲמָן הוּא יְזַכֵּנוּ לִימוֹת הַמָּשִׁיחַ וּלְחַיֵּי הָעוֹלָם הַבָּא

He who is merciful shall reign over us forever.
He who is merciful shall be blessed in the heavens and on earth.
He who is merciful shall be praised for generations, and shall be proud of us for eternity, and boast of us until the end of days.
He who is merciful shall provide for us honorably.
He who is merciful shall break the yoke of exile from our neck and lead us to our land.
He who is merciful shall shower us with blessings in this home and on this table at which we have eaten.
He who is merciful shall send to us Elijah the prophet who is kindly remembered, and bring us good tidings, salvation, and consolation.

   Add on Shabbat:

(He who is merciful shall grant us a day that is entirely Shabbat and rest forever more.)
He who is merciful shall grant us a day that is all good.
He who is merciful shall grant us the privilege of seeing the days of the Messiah and a life in the world to come.

מִגְדוֹל יְשׁוּעוֹת מַלְכּוֹ, וְעֹשֶׂה חֶסֶד לִמְשִׁיחוֹ, לְדָוִד וּלְזַרְעוֹ עַד עוֹלָם. עֹשֶׂה שָׁלוֹם בִּמְרוֹמָיו, הוּא יַעֲשֶׂה שָׁלוֹם עָלֵינוּ וְעַל כָּל יִשְׂרָאֵל. וְאִמְרוּ: "אָמֵן".

He is our tower of salvation, He is charitable with His Messiah, David, and his descendants. He who makes peace in the heavens will make peace among us and among all the people of Israel. And say, "Amen".

יְראוּ אֶת יְיָ קְדֹשָׁיו, כִּי אֵין מַחְסוֹר לִירֵאָיו. כְּפִירִים רָשׁוּ וְרָעֵבוּ, וְדֹרְשֵׁי יְיָ לֹא יַחְסְרוּ כָל טוֹב. הוֹדוּ לַיְיָ כִּי טוֹב, כִּי

לְעוֹלָם חַסְדּוֹ. פּוֹתֵחַ אֶת יָדֶךָ, וּמַשְׂבִּיעַ לְכָל חַי רָצוֹן. בָּרוּךְ הַגֶּבֶר אֲשֶׁר יִבְטַח בַּיְיָ, וְהָיָה יְיָ מִבְטַחוֹ. נַעַר הָיִיתִי גַם זָקַנְתִּי, וְלֹא רָאִיתִי צַדִּיק נֶעֱזָב, וְזַרְעוֹ מְבַקֶּשׁ לָחֶם. יְיָ עֹז לְעַמּוֹ יִתֵּן, יְיָ יְבָרֵךְ אֶת עַמּוֹ בַשָּׁלוֹם.

Revere the Lord, you who are His holy ones, for those who do lack for nothing. Lions have starved yet G-d's believers never shall. Thank G-d for He is good, and His charity is eternal. You open Your hand and satisfy the desires of every living thing. Blessed is he who trusts in G-d and who puts his trust in G-d. A boy I once was, now I have grown old, but I have never seen a righteous man forgotten, nor his children wanting for bread. G-d will give strength to His people, G-d will bless His people with peace.

Hallel

לֹא לָנוּ יְיָ לֹא לָנוּ, כִּי לְשִׁמְךָ תֵּן כָּבוֹד, עַל חַסְדְּךָ, עַל אֲמִתֶּךָ. לָמָּה יֹאמְרוּ הַגּוֹיִם אַיֵּה נָא אֱלֹהֵיהֶם, וֵאלֹהֵינוּ בַשָּׁמַיִם, כֹּל אֲשֶׁר חָפֵץ עָשָׂה. עֲצַבֵּיהֶם כֶּסֶף וְזָהָב מַעֲשֵׂה יְדֵי אָדָם. פֶּה לָהֶם וְלֹא יְדַבֵּרוּ, עֵינַיִם לָהֶם וְלֹא יִרְאוּ. אָזְנַיִם לָהֶם וְלֹא יִשְׁמָעוּ, אַף לָהֶם וְלֹא יְרִיחוּן. יְדֵיהֶם וְלֹא יְמִישׁוּן, רַגְלֵיהֶם וְלֹא יְהַלֵּכוּ, לֹא יֶהְגּוּ בִּגְרוֹנָם. כְּמוֹהֶם יִהְיוּ עֹשֵׂיהֶם, כֹּל אֲשֶׁר בֹּטֵחַ בָּהֶם. יִשְׂרָאֵל בְּטַח בַּיְיָ, עֶזְרָם וּמָגִנָּם הוּא. בֵּית אַהֲרֹן בִּטְחוּ בַיְיָ, עֶזְרָם וּמָגִנָּם הוּא. יִרְאֵי יְיָ בִּטְחוּ בַיְיָ, עֶזְרָם וּמָגִנָּם הוּא.

Not to us, Lord, not to us, but to Your Name give glory, in recognition of Your kindness and Your truth. Why should the nations ask, "Where is their god?" Our G-d is in heaven, He does what He desires. Their manmade idols are of silver and gold. They have a mouth, but cannot speak; they have eyes, but cannot see; they have ears, but cannot hear; they have a nose, but cannot smell; their hands cannot feel; their legs cannot walk; no sound comes from their throat. May their makers and everyone that believes in them be like them. Israel, trust in the Lord! He is your help and your savior. House of Aaron, trust in the Lord! He is your help and your savior. You who fear the Lord, trust in the Lord! He is your help and your savior.

יְיָ זְכָרָנוּ יְבָרֵךְ, יְבָרֵךְ אֶת בֵּית יִשְׂרָאֵל, יְבָרֵךְ אֶת בֵּית אַהֲרֹן. יְבָרֵךְ יִרְאֵי יְיָ, הַקְּטַנִּים עִם הַגְּדֹלִים. יֹסֵף יְיָ עֲלֵיכֶם, עֲלֵיכֶם וְעַל בְּנֵיכֶם. בְּרוּכִים אַתֶּם לַיְיָ, עֹשֵׂה שָׁמַיִם וָאָרֶץ. הַשָּׁמַיִם שָׁמַיִם לַיְיָ, וְהָאָרֶץ נָתַן לִבְנֵי אָדָם. לֹא הַמֵּתִים יְהַלְלוּ יָהּ וְלֹא כָּל יֹרְדֵי דוּמָה. וַאֲנַחְנוּ נְבָרֵךְ יָהּ מֵעַתָּה וְעַד עוֹלָם. הַלְלוּיָהּ:

Lord, remember us and bless us. Bless the House of Israel; bless the House of Aaron; bless those who fear Him, the small and the great. May the Lord add to your blessings and those of your children. You are welcomed by the Lord, creator of heaven and earth. The heavens belong to G-d, but the earth He gave to the sons of man. The dead do not praise G-d, nor do those that go down into the silence of the grave. But we will bless G-d, from now to eternity. Halleluyah.

אָהַבְתִּי כִּי יִשְׁמַע יְיָ אֶת קוֹלִי, תַּחֲנוּנָי. כִּי הִטָּה אָזְנוֹ לִי וּבְיָמַי אֶקְרָא. אֲפָפוּנִי חֶבְלֵי מָוֶת וּמְצָרֵי שְׁאוֹל מְצָאוּנִי, צָרָה וְיָגוֹן אֶמְצָא. וּבְשֵׁם יְיָ אֶקְרָא, אָנָּא יְיָ מַלְּטָה נַפְשִׁי. חַנּוּן יְיָ וְצַדִּיק, וֵאלֹהֵינוּ מְרַחֵם. שֹׁמֵר פְּתָאִים יְיָ, דַּלּוֹתִי וְלִי יְהוֹשִׁיעַ. שׁוּבִי נַפְשִׁי לִמְנוּחָיְכִי, כִּי יְיָ גָּמַל עָלָיְכִי. כִּי חִלַּצְתָּ נַפְשִׁי מִמָּוֶת, אֶת עֵינִי מִן דִּמְעָה, אֶת רַגְלִי מִדֶּחִי. אֶתְהַלֵּךְ לִפְנֵי יְיָ בְּאַרְצוֹת הַחַיִּים. הֶאֱמַנְתִּי כִּי אֲדַבֵּר, אֲנִי עָנִיתִי מְאֹד. אֲנִי אָמַרְתִּי בְחָפְזִי, כָּל הָאָדָם כֹּזֵב.

I love the Lord, for He hears my voice and my prayers. For He turned His ear to me and I will call for Him every day. The grip of death shall enfold me and the agonies of the grave may find me, trouble and sorrow I shall encounter. I call the Name of G-d: Please, Lord, deliver my soul. G-d is gracious and just, G-d is compassionate. The Lord watches over the simpletons; I was brought low and He saved me. Return, my soul, to your rest, for the Lord has been kind to you. For You have saved my soul from death, my eyes from tears, my feet from falling. I will walk before You, G-d, in the land of the living. Even in my darkest times, I did not cease to believe. Even when I said in haste, "All men are deceitful."

מָה אָשִׁיב לַייָ כָּל תַּגְמוּלוֹהִי עָלָי. כּוֹס יְשׁוּעוֹת אֶשָּׂא וּבְשֵׁם יְיָ אֶקְרָא. נְדָרַי לַייָ אֲשַׁלֵּם נֶגְדָה נָּא לְכָל עַמּוֹ. יָקָר בְּעֵינֵי יְיָ הַמָּוְתָה לַחֲסִידָיו. אָנָּא יְיָ כִּי אֲנִי עַבְדֶּךָ, אֲנִי עַבְדְּךָ בֶּן

אֲמָתֶךָ, פִּתַּחְתָּ לְמוֹסֵרָי. לְךָ אֶזְבַּח זֶבַח תּוֹדָה וּבְשֵׁם יְיָ אֶקְרָא. נְדָרַי לַיְיָ אֲשַׁלֵּם נֶגְדָה נָּא לְכָל עַמּוֹ. בְּחַצְרוֹת בֵּית יְיָ, בְּתוֹכֵכִי יְרוּשָׁלָיִם, הַלְלוּיָהּ:

How might I repay the Lord for all that He has done for me? I will raise a cup of salvation and call the Name of the Lord. I will pay my vows to the Lord in the presence of all His people. Precious in the eyes of G-d is the death of His pious ones. Lord, I am Your servant, I am Your servant the son of Your handmaid, You have freed me from my chains. To You I will bring an offering of thanksgiving, and I will call Your Name. I will pay my vows to the Lord in the presence of all His people, in the courtyards of the House of G-d, in the heart of Jerusalem. Halleluyah.

הַלְלוּ אֶת יְיָ כָּל גּוֹיִם, שַׁבְּחוּהוּ כָּל הָאֻמִּים. כִּי גָבַר עָלֵינוּ חַסְדּוֹ, וֶאֱמֶת יְיָ לְעוֹלָם, הַלְלוּיָהּ:

Praise the Lord, all nations, commend Him, all peoples. For His kindness is mighty over us, and His truth is eternal. Halleluyah.

הוֹדוּ לַיְיָ כִּי טוֹב כִּי לְעוֹלָם חַסְדּוֹ.
יֹאמַר נָא יִשְׂרָאֵל כִּי לְעוֹלָם חַסְדּוֹ.
יֹאמְרוּ נָא בֵית אַהֲרֹן כִּי לְעוֹלָם חַסְדּוֹ.
יֹאמְרוּ נָא יִרְאֵי יְיָ כִּי לְעוֹלָם חַסְדּוֹ.

Give thanks to the L-rd, for He is good, for His kindness is everlasting.
Let Israel say it, for His kindness is everlasting.
Let the House of Aaron say it, for His kindness is everlasting.
Let those who fear the L-rd say it, for His kindness is everlasting

מִן הַמֵּצַר קָרָאתִי יָּהּ, עָנָנִי בַמֶּרְחָב יָהּ.
יְיָ לִי לֹא אִירָא, מַה יַּעֲשֶׂה לִי אָדָם.
יְיָ לִי בְּעֹזְרָי וַאֲנִי אֶרְאֶה בְשֹׂנְאָי.

ADDITIONS

טוֹב לַחֲסוֹת בַּייָ מִבְּטֹחַ בָּאָדָם.
טוֹב לַחֲסוֹת בַּייָ מִבְּטֹחַ בִּנְדִיבִים.
כָּל גּוֹיִם סְבָבוּנִי, בְּשֵׁם יְיָ כִּי אֲמִילַם.
סַבּוּנִי גַם סְבָבוּנִי, בְּשֵׁם יְיָ כִּי אֲמִילַם.
סַבּוּנִי כִדְבֹרִים, דֹּעֲכוּ כְּאֵשׁ קוֹצִים, בְּשֵׁם יְיָ כִּי אֲמִילַם.
דָּחֹה דְחִיתַנִי לִנְפֹּל, וַייָ עֲזָרָנִי.
עָזִּי וְזִמְרָת יָהּ וַיְהִי לִי לִישׁוּעָה.
קוֹל רִנָּה וִישׁוּעָה בְּאָהֳלֵי צַדִּיקִים, יְמִין יְיָ עֹשָׂה חָיִל.
יְמִין יְיָ רוֹמֵמָה, יְמִין יְיָ עֹשָׂה חָיִל.
לֹא אָמוּת כִּי אֶחְיֶה, וַאֲסַפֵּר מַעֲשֵׂי יָהּ.
יַסֹּר יִסְּרַנִי יָהּ, וְלַמָּוֶת לֹא נְתָנָנִי.
פִּתְחוּ לִי שַׁעֲרֵי צֶדֶק, אָבֹא בָם, אוֹדֶה יָהּ.
זֶה הַשַּׁעַר לַייָ, צַדִּיקִים יָבֹאוּ בוֹ.
אוֹדְךָ כִּי עֲנִיתָנִי וַתְּהִי לִי לִישׁוּעָה.
אוֹדְךָ כִּי עֲנִיתָנִי וַתְּהִי לִי לִישׁוּעָה.
אֶבֶן מָאֲסוּ הַבּוֹנִים הָיְתָה לְרֹאשׁ פִּנָּה.
אֶבֶן מָאֲסוּ הַבּוֹנִים הָיְתָה לְרֹאשׁ פִּנָּה.
מֵאֵת יְיָ הָיְתָה זֹּאת הִיא נִפְלָאת בְּעֵינֵינוּ.
זֶה הַיּוֹם עָשָׂה יְיָ נָגִילָה וְנִשְׂמְחָה בוֹ.

Out of narrow straits I called to G-d; and G-d answered me.
The Lord is with me, I will not fear what man can do to me.
The Lord is my helper, and I can face my enemies.
It is better to rely on the Lord, than to trust in man.
It is better to rely on the Lord, than to trust in nobles.
All nations surround me, but I cut them down in the Name of the Lord.
They surrounded me, but I cut them down in the Name of the Lord.
They surrounded me like bees, yet they are extinguished like a fire to thorns; I cut them down in the Name of the Lord.
My enemies pushed me down again and again, but the Lord helped me.

G-d is my strength and song, my salvation.
Sounds of song and salvation are heard in the tents of the righteous:
"The right hand of the Lord performs deeds of valor.
The right hand of the Lord is exalted; the right hand of the Lord performs deeds of valor!"
I shall not die, but I shall live and relate the deeds of G-d.
G-d has chastised me, but He has not given me over to death.
Open the gates of righteousness; I will enter them and give thanks to G-d.
This is the gate of the Lord, the righteous will enter it.
I thank You for You have answered me, and You have been a help to me.
The stone neglected by the builders is now the cornerstone.
This was the doing of the Lord, miraculous in our eyes.
For what the Lord has done this day, let us be glad and rejoice.

אָנָּא יְיָ, הוֹשִׁיעָה נָּא.
אָנָּא יְיָ, הַצְלִיחָה נָא

Lord, please save us.

Lord, please aid us.

בָּרוּךְ הַבָּא בְּשֵׁם יְיָ, בֵּרַכְנוּכֶם מִבֵּית יְיָ. בָּרוּךְ הַבָּא בְּשֵׁם יְיָ, בֵּרַכְנוּכֶם מִבֵּית יְיָ. אֵל יְיָ וַיָּאֶר לָנוּ. אִסְרוּ חַג בַּעֲבֹתִים עַד קַרְנוֹת הַמִּזְבֵּחַ. אֵל יְיָ וַיָּאֶר לָנוּ. אִסְרוּ חַג בַּעֲבֹתִים עַד קַרְנוֹת הַמִּזְבֵּחַ. אֵלִי אַתָּה וְאוֹדֶךָּ, אֱלֹהַי אֲרוֹמְמֶךָּ. אֵלִי אַתָּה וְאוֹדֶךָּ, אֱלֹהַי אֲרוֹמְמֶךָּ. הוֹדוּ לַיְיָ כִּי טוֹב, כִּי לְעוֹלָם חַסְדּוֹ. הוֹדוּ לַיְיָ כִּי טוֹב, כִּי לְעוֹלָם חַסְדּוֹ.

Blessed is he who comes in the Name of the Lord, we welcome you from the House of the Lord. The Lord is Almighty, He gave us light;

bind the festival offering for the altar. You are my G-d and I will thank You; my G-d, I will praise You. Give thanks to the Lord, for He is good, for His goodness is eternal.

יְהַלְלוּךָ יי אֱלֹהֵינוּ כָּל מַעֲשֶׂיךָ, וַחֲסִידֶיךָ צַדִּיקִים עוֹשֵׂי רְצוֹנֶךָ, וְכָל עַמְּךָ בֵּית יִשְׂרָאֵל בְּרִנָּה יוֹדוּ וִיבָרְכוּ, וִישַׁבְּחוּ וִיפָאֲרוּ, וִירוֹמְמוּ וְיַעֲרִיצוּ, וְיַקְדִּישׁוּ וְיַמְלִיכוּ אֶת שִׁמְךָ, מַלְכֵּנוּ. כִּי לְךָ טוֹב לְהוֹדוֹת וּלְשִׁמְךָ נָאֶה לְזַמֵּר, כִּי מֵעוֹלָם וְעַד עוֹלָם אַתָּה אֵל.

Lord, our G-d, all Your creations shall praise You; Your pious ones, the righteous who do Your will, and all Your people, the House of Israel, with joyous song will thank and bless, praise and glorify, exalt and admire, sanctify and proclaim the sovereignty of Your Name, our King. For it is good to thank You, and Your Name warrants song, You have always been and will always be G-d.

הוֹדוּ לַאֲדֹנֵי הָאֲדֹנִים - כִּי לְעוֹלָם חַסְדּוֹ
לְעֹשֵׂה נִפְלָאוֹת גְּדֹלוֹת לְבַדּוֹ - כִּי לְעוֹלָם חַסְדּוֹ
לְעֹשֵׂה הַשָּׁמַיִם בִּתְבוּנָה - כִּי לְעוֹלָם חַסְדּוֹ
לְרוֹקַע הָאָרֶץ עַל הַמָּיִם - כִּי לְעוֹלָם חַסְדּוֹ
לְעֹשֵׂה אוֹרִים גְּדֹלִים - כִּי לְעוֹלָם חַסְדּוֹ
אֶת הַשֶּׁמֶשׁ לְמֶמְשֶׁלֶת בַּיּוֹם - כִּי לְעוֹלָם חַסְדּוֹ
אֶת הַיָּרֵחַ וְכוֹכָבִים לְמֶמְשְׁלוֹת בַּלָּיְלָה - כִּי לְעוֹלָם חַסְדּוֹ
לְמַכֵּה מִצְרַיִם בִּבְכוֹרֵיהֶם - כִּי לְעוֹלָם חַסְדּוֹ
וַיּוֹצֵא יִשְׂרָאֵל מִתּוֹכָם - כִּי לְעוֹלָם חַסְדּוֹ
בְּיָד חֲזָקָה וּבִזְרוֹעַ נְטוּיָה - כִּי לְעוֹלָם חַסְדּוֹ
לְגֹזֵר יַם סוּף לִגְזָרִים - כִּי לְעוֹלָם חַסְדּוֹ
וְהֶעֱבִיר יִשְׂרָאֵל בְּתוֹכוֹ - כִּי לְעוֹלָם חַסְדּוֹ
וְנִעֵר פַּרְעֹה וְחֵילוֹ בְיַם סוּף - כִּי לְעוֹלָם חַסְדּוֹ
לְמוֹלִיךְ עַמּוֹ בַּמִּדְבָּר - כִּי לְעוֹלָם חַסְדּוֹ

לְמַכֵּה מְלָכִים גְּדֹלִים - כִּי לְעוֹלָם חַסְדּוֹ
וַיַּהֲרֹג מְלָכִים אַדִּירִים - כִּי לְעוֹלָם חַסְדּוֹ
לְסִיחוֹן מֶלֶךְ הָאֱמֹרִי - כִּי לְעוֹלָם חַסְדּוֹ
וּלְעוֹג מֶלֶךְ הַבָּשָׁן - כִּי לְעוֹלָם חַסְדּוֹ
וְנָתַן אַרְצָם לְנַחֲלָה - כִּי לְעוֹלָם חַסְדּוֹ
נַחֲלָה לְיִשְׂרָאֵל עַבְדּוֹ - כִּי לְעוֹלָם חַסְדּוֹ
שֶׁבְּשִׁפְלֵנוּ זָכַר לָנוּ - כִּי לְעוֹלָם חַסְדּוֹ
וַיִּפְרְקֵנוּ מִצָּרֵינוּ - כִּי לְעוֹלָם חַסְדּוֹ
נֹתֵן לֶחֶם לְכָל בָּשָׂר - כִּי לְעוֹלָם חַסְדּוֹ
הוֹדוּ לְאֵל הַשָּׁמָיִם - כִּי לְעוֹלָם חַסְדּוֹ

Give thanks to the Lord of lords — for His goodness is eternal;
Who alone does great wonders — for His goodness is eternal;
Who made the heavens with understanding — for His goodness is eternal;
Who stretched the earth above the waters — for His goodness is eternal;
Who made the great lights — for His goodness is eternal;
The sun, to rule by day for — His goodness is eternal;
The moon and stars, to rule by night — for His goodness is eternal;
Who struck Egypt's first-born — for His goodness is eternal;
And brought Israel out of their midst — for His goodness is eternal;
With a strong hand and with an outstretched arm — for His goodness is eternal;
Who split the Sea of Reeds — for His goodness is eternal;
And led Israel through it — for His goodness is eternal;
And cast Pharaoh and his army into the Sea of Reeds — for His goodness is eternal;
Who led His people through the desert — for His goodness is eternal;
Who struck great kings — for His goodness is eternal;
And slew mighty kings — for His goodness is eternal;
Sichon, king of the Amorites — for His goodness is eternal;

And Og, king of Bashan — for His goodness is eternal;
And gave their land as a heritage — for His goodness is eternal;
A heritage to Israel, His servant — for His goodness is eternal;
Who remembered us in our lowliness — for His goodness is eternal;
And delivered us from our oppressors — for His goodness is eternal;
Who gives food to every living thing — for His goodness is eternal;
Thank the G-d of the heavens for His goodness is eternal.

Nishmat Kol Chai

נִשְׁמַת כָּל חַי תְּבָרֵךְ אֶת שִׁמְךָ יְהֹוָה אֱלֹהֵינוּ. וְרוּחַ כָּל בָּשָׂר תְּפָאֵר וּתְרוֹמֵם זִכְרְךָ מַלְכֵּנוּ תָּמִיד. מִן הָעוֹלָם וְעַד הָעוֹלָם אַתָּה אֵל. וּמִבַּלְעָדֶיךָ אֵין לָנוּ מֶלֶךְ גּוֹאֵל וּמוֹשִׁיעַ. פּוֹדֶה וּמַצִּיל וּמְפַרְנֵס וּמְרַחֵם בְּכָל עֵת צָרָה וְצוּקָה. אֵין לָנוּ מֶלֶךְ עוֹזֵר וְסוֹמֵךְ אֶלָּא אָתָּה. אֱלֹהֵי הָרִאשׁוֹנִים וְהָאַחֲרוֹנִים, אֱלוֹהַּ כָּל בְּרִיּוֹת, אֲדוֹן כָּל תּוֹלָדוֹת, הַמְהֻלָּל בְּרוֹב הַתִּשְׁבָּחוֹת, הַמְנַהֵג עוֹלָמוֹ בְּחֶסֶד וּבְרִיּוֹתָיו בְּרַחֲמִים. וַיהֹוָה לֹא יָנוּם וְלֹא יִישָׁן, הַמְעוֹרֵר יְשֵׁנִים, וְהַמֵּקִיץ נִרְדָּמִים, וְהַמֵּשִׂיחַ אִלְּמִים, וְהַמַּתִּיר אֲסוּרִים, וְהַסּוֹמֵךְ נוֹפְלִים, וְהַזּוֹקֵף כְּפוּפִים, לְךָ לְבַדְּךָ אֲנַחְנוּ מוֹדִים. אִלּוּ פִינוּ מָלֵא שִׁירָה כַּיָּם, וּלְשׁוֹנֵנוּ רִנָּה כַּהֲמוֹן גַּלָּיו, וְשִׂפְתוֹתֵינוּ שֶׁבַח כְּמֶרְחֲבֵי רָקִיעַ, וְעֵינֵינוּ מְאִירוֹת כַּשֶּׁמֶשׁ וְכַיָּרֵחַ, וְיָדֵינוּ פְרוּשׂוֹת כְּנִשְׁרֵי שָׁמָיִם, וְרַגְלֵינוּ קַלּוֹת כָּאַיָּלוֹת, אֵין אֲנַחְנוּ מַסְפִּיקִים לְהוֹדוֹת לְךָ יְהֹוָה אֱלֹהֵינוּ וֵאלֹהֵי אֲבוֹתֵינוּ, וּלְבָרֵךְ אֶת שִׁמְךָ עַל אַחַת מֵאֶלֶף אַלְפֵי אֲלָפִים וְרִבֵּי רְבָבוֹת פְּעָמִים, הַטּוֹבוֹת שֶׁעָשִׂיתָ עִם אֲבוֹתֵינוּ וְעִמָּנוּ. מִמִּצְרַיִם גְּאַלְתָּנוּ יְהֹוָה אֱלֹהֵינוּ וּמִבֵּית עֲבָדִים פְּדִיתָנוּ, בְּרָעָב זַנְתָּנוּ, וּבְשָׂבָע כִּלְכַּלְתָּנוּ; מֵחֶרֶב הִצַּלְתָּנוּ, וּמִדֶּבֶר מִלַּטְתָּנוּ, וּמֵחֳלָיִם רָעִים וְנֶאֱמָנִים דִּלִּיתָנוּ. עַד הֵנָּה עֲזָרוּנוּ רַחֲמֶיךָ, וְלֹא עֲזָבוּנוּ חֲסָדֶיךָ וְאַל תִּטְּשֵׁנוּ יְהֹוָה אֱלֹהֵינוּ לָנֶצַח. עַל כֵּן אֵבָרִים שֶׁפִּלַּגְתָּ בָּנוּ, וְרוּחַ וּנְשָׁמָה שֶׁנָּפַחְתָּ בְּאַפֵּינוּ, וְלָשׁוֹן אֲשֶׁר שַׂמְתָּ בְּפִינוּ, הֵן הֵם יוֹדוּ וִיבָרְכוּ וִישַׁבְּחוּ וִיפָאֲרוּ וִירוֹמְמוּ וְיַעֲרִיצוּ וְיַקְדִּישׁוּ וְיַמְלִיכוּ אֶת שִׁמְךָ מַלְכֵּנוּ. כִּי כָל פֶּה לְךָ יוֹדֶה, וְכָל לָשׁוֹן לְךָ תִשָּׁבַע, וְכָל בֶּרֶךְ לְךָ תִכְרַע, וְכָל קוֹמָה לְפָנֶיךָ תִשְׁתַּחֲוֶה, וְכָל לְבָבוֹת יִירָאוּךָ, וְכָל קֶרֶב וּכְלָיוֹת יְזַמְּרוּ לִשְׁמֶךָ. כַּדָּבָר שֶׁכָּתוּב: כָּל עַצְמוֹתַי תֹּאמַרְנָה יְהֹוָה מִי כָמוֹךָ, מַצִּיל עָנִי

מְחַזֵּק מִמֶּנּוּ, וְעָנִי וְאֶבְיוֹן מִגֹּזְלוֹ. מִי יִדְמֶה לָּךְ, וּמִי יִשְׁוֶה לָּךְ, וּמִי יַעֲרָךְ לָךְ, הָאֵל הַגָּדוֹל הַגִּבּוֹר וְהַנּוֹרָא אֵל עֶלְיוֹן, קוֹנֵה שָׁמַיִם וָאָרֶץ. נְהַלֶּלְךָ וּנְשַׁבֵּחֲךָ וּנְפָאֶרְךָ וּנְבָרֵךְ אֶת שֵׁם קָדְשֶׁךָ, כָּאָמוּר: לְדָוִד, בָּרְכִי נַפְשִׁי אֶת יְהֹוָה, וְכָל קְרָבַי אֶת שֵׁם קָדְשׁוֹ: הָאֵל בְּתַעֲצֻמוֹת עֻזֶּךָ, הַגָּדוֹל בִּכְבוֹד שְׁמֶךָ, הַגִּבּוֹר לָנֶצַח וְהַנּוֹרָא בְּנוֹרְאוֹתֶיךָ. הַמֶּלֶךְ הַיּוֹשֵׁב עַל כִּסֵּא רָם וְנִשָּׂא. שׁוֹכֵן עַד מָרוֹם וְקָדוֹשׁ שְׁמוֹ. וְכָתוּב רַנְּנוּ צַדִּיקִים בַּיהֹוָה, לַיְשָׁרִים נָאוָה תְהִלָּה. בְּפִי יְשָׁרִים תִּתְהַלָּל, וּבְדִבְרֵי צַדִּיקִים תִּתְבָּרַךְ, וּבִלְשׁוֹן חֲסִידִים תִּתְרוֹמָם, וּבְקֶרֶב קְדוֹשִׁים תִּתְקַדָּשׁ. וּבְמַקְהֲלוֹת רִבְבוֹת עַמְּךָ בֵּית יִשְׂרָאֵל, בְּרִנָּה יִתְפָּאֵר שִׁמְךָ מַלְכֵּנוּ בְּכָל דּוֹר וָדוֹר, שֶׁכֵּן חוֹבַת כָּל הַיְצוּרִים, לְפָנֶיךָ יְהֹוָה אֱלֹהֵינוּ וֵאלֹהֵי אֲבוֹתֵינוּ, לְהוֹדוֹת לְהַלֵּל לְשַׁבֵּחַ לְפָאֵר לְרוֹמֵם לְהַדֵּר לְבָרֵךְ לְעַלֵּה וּלְקַלֵּס, עַל כָּל דִּבְרֵי שִׁירוֹת וְתִשְׁבְּחוֹת דָּוִד בֶּן יִשַׁי עַבְדְּךָ מְשִׁיחֶךָ: וּבְכֵן יִשְׁתַּבַּח שִׁמְךָ לָעַד מַלְכֵּנוּ, הָאֵל, הַמֶּלֶךְ הַגָּדוֹל, וְהַקָּדוֹשׁ, בַּשָּׁמַיִם וּבָאָרֶץ. כִּי לְךָ נָאֶה יְהֹוָה אֱלֹהֵינוּ וֵאלֹהֵי אֲבוֹתֵינוּ שִׁיר וּשְׁבָחָה, הַלֵּל וְזִמְרָה, עֹז וּמֶמְשָׁלָה, נֶצַח, גְּדֻלָּה וּגְבוּרָה תְּהִלָּה וְתִפְאֶרֶת, קְדֻשָּׁה, וּמַלְכוּת. בְּרָכוֹת, וְהוֹדָאוֹת, לְשִׁמְךָ הַגָּדוֹל, וְהַקָּדוֹשׁ, וּמֵעוֹלָם וְעַד עוֹלָם אַתָּה אֵל: בָּרוּךְ אַתָּה יְהֹוָה, אֵל מֶלֶךְ, גָּדוֹל וּמְהֻלָּל בַּתִּשְׁבָּחוֹת, אֵל הַהוֹדָאוֹת, אֲדוֹן הַנִּפְלָאוֹת, בּוֹרֵא כָּל הַנְּשָׁמוֹת, רִבּוֹן כָּל הַמַּעֲשִׂים, הַבּוֹחֵר בְּשִׁירֵי זִמְרָה, מֶלֶךְ יָחִיד אֵל, חֵי הָעוֹלָמִים:

The soul of every living being shall bless Your Name, Lord our God, the spirit of all flesh shall always glorify and exalt Your remembrance, our King. From this world to the World to Come, You are God, and other than You we have no king, redeemer, or savior. He who liberates, rescues and sustains, answers and is merciful in every time of distress and anguish, we have no king, helper or supporter but You! God of the first and the last, God of all creatures, Master of all Generations, Who is extolled through a multitude of praises, Who guides His world with kindness and His creatures with mercy. G-d is truth; He neither slumbers nor sleeps. He Who rouses the sleepers and awakens the slumberers. Who raises the dead and heals the sick, causes the blind to see and straightens the bent. Who makes the mute speak and reveals what is hidden. To You alone we give thanks! Were our mouth as full of song as the sea, and our tongue as full of joyous song as its multitude of waves, and our lips as full of praise as the breadth of the heavens, and our eyes as brilliant as the sun and the moon, and our hands as outspread as the eagles of the sky and our feet as swift as hinds — we still could not thank You sufficiently, Lord our God and God of our forefathers, and to bless Your Name for even one of the thousand thousand, thousands of thousands and myriad myriads of favors, miracles and wonders that You performed for our ancestors and for us. At first You redeemed us from Egypt, Lord our God, and liberated us from the house of bondage. In famine You nourished us, and in plenty You sustained us. From sword You saved us; from plague You let us escape; and from severe and enduring diseases You spared us. Until now Your mercy has helped us, and Your kindness has not forsaken us. Do not abandon us, Lord our God, forever. Therefore the organs that You set within us and the spirit and soul that You breathed into our nostrils, and the tongue that You placed in our mouth - all of them shall thank and bless and praise and glorify, exalt and revere, be devoted, sanctify and declare the sovereignty of Your Name, our King. For every mouth shall offer thanks to You; every tongue shall vow allegiance to You; every knee shall bend to You; every erect spine shall prostrate itself before You; all hearts shall fear You; and all innermost feelings and thoughts shall sing praises to Your name, as it is written: "All my bones shall say, G-d who is like You? You save the poor man from one who is stronger than he, the poor and destitute from the one who would rob him." The outcry of the poor You hear, the screams of the destitute You listen to, and You save. And it is written: "Sing joyfully, O righteous, before G-d; for the upright praise is fitting." By the mouth of the upright You shall be exalted; By the lips of the righteous shall You be blessed; By the tongue of the devout shall You be sanctified; And amid the holy shall You be lauded. And in the assemblies of the myriads of Your people, the House of Israel, it is the duty of all creatures, before You O G-d, our God and God of our forefathers to thank, laud, praise, glorify, exalt, adore, render triumphant, bless, raise high, and sing praises - even beyond all expressions of the songs and praises of David, the son of Jesse, Your servant, Your anointed. And thus may Your name be praised forever- our King, the God, the Great and holy King - in heaven and on earth. Because for You it is fitting - O G-d our God and God of our forefathers — song and praise, lauding and hymns, power and dominion, triumph, greatness and strength, praise and splendor, holiness and sovereignty, blessings and thanksgivings to Your Great and Holy Name; from this world to the world to come You are God.

www.ingramcontent.com/pod-product-compliance
Lightning Source LLC
LaVergne TN
LVHW020425070526
838199LV00003B/283